THE ENLIGHTENMENT PROCESS

A Guide to Embodied Spiritual Awakening

THE ENLIGHTENMENT PROCESS

A Guide to Embodied Spiritual Awakening

JUDITH BLACKSTONE

PARAGON HOUSE
St. Paul, Minnesota

Published in the United States by
Paragon House
1925 Oakcrest Avenue
St. Paul, MN 55113

Copyright ©2008 Paragon House

Library of Congress Cataloging-in-Publication Data

Blackstone, Judith, 1947-
  The enlightenment process : a guide to embodied spiritual awakening / by
Judith Blackstone.
      p. cm.
  Summary: "Describes the process of spiritual enlightenment using
meditational and physical exercises that can help deepen spiritual
awareness, develop the capacity to connect with others and reconnect with
the world"--Provided by publisher.
  Includes bibliographical references (p.   ) and index.
  ISBN-13: 978-1-55778-873-3 (pbk. : alk. paper)
  1. Spiritual life. 2. Self-realization. 3. Spiritual exercises. I.
Title.
  BL624.B524 2008
  204'.2--dc22
                          2007044137

Manufactured in the United States of America

The paper used in this publication meets the minimum requirements of American
National Standard for Information Sciences—Permanence of Paper for Printed
Library Materials, ANSIZ39.48-1984.

10 9 8 7 6 5 4 3 2 1

              For current information about all releases from Paragon House,
                 visit the web site at http://www.paragonhouse.com

Acknowledgments

I offer my deepest thanks to my husband, Zoran Josipovic, and to Meg Lundstrom, for their encouragement, advice, and precious company as I wrote and rewrote this book. And to my many teachers and healers, and my students, whose courage and wisdom inspire me every day.

Contents

Preface. ix

Introduction. xi

1 Describing Enlightenment 1

2 Self and Selflessness 27

3 The Healing Process 63

4 Distance and Intimacy 83

5 The Body of Clear Space 111

6 Person and Cosmos 135

Epilogue 157

References 159

Index to the Exercises 163

Index 165

Preface

Although enlightenment is no more mysterious than many other human experiences, such as our ability to love or to create, it is more rare. It only occurs as we reach a particular degree of sensitivity or openness to life. Most books about spirituality focus on more common spiritual experiences, such as the ability to feel compassion for other people, or to be attentive to the present moment. Yet I have found that many people are capable, with some practice, of the experience described here. This is the realization, or unveiling, of a subtle dimension of consciousness pervading our own being and everything around us as a unified whole. It is the experience of the luminous transparency of ourselves and our environment, and the fullness and vividness of being that occurs with it.

The revisions in this book (first published in 1997) reflect my endeavor to more clearly describe enlightenment and its relationship to psychological healing and embodiment, and to address questions that readers of the first edition have posed to me. My most difficult decision in presenting this new edition was whether or not to change the title. I chose to keep the title after a long debate with myself about the merits of the word "enlightenment." Although this word is generally associated, in the Asian spiritual texts, with the type of experience I am describing, it has many other popular uses. And for many people, it signifies an extremely advanced, virtually inaccessible state of spiritual attainment. However, I also thought that it was important to preserve some of the mystical quality that this word implies. One of the changes that has occurred since I first wrote this book is that Asian spiritual ideas and practices have become more widely accepted in the West, entering both our mainstream popular culture and our scientific and philosophical communities. This means that descriptions of spiritual experiences are regarded as somewhat more valid than in the past. But there may also be a drawback to this growing popularity. That is, we may, as a society, reduce the Asian knowledge of our spiritual potential to something more palatable to Western taste, something that does not present too much of a challenge to contemporary Western beliefs. I chose to keep the word "enlightenment" in the title and in the following text in order to express that this experience, although accessible to anyone interested in it, leads beyond what we can grasp with our intellect or our technology.

Contrary to the basic tenets of contemporary Western philosophy, the experience of our fundamental, unified dimension of consciousness is uncreated; it arises spontaneously as we relinquish our constraints on ourselves. Enlightenment is the laying bare of our own human nature, and yet it is extraordinary. It means to experience oneself and the world as made of the light of consciousness. I hope to convey, in the following pages, both the accessibility and the preciousness of this experience.

Introduction

Enlightenment is often spoken of as awakening. But what do we awaken to? How does enlightenment transform our experience of our environment, other people, the cosmos, and our own self? This book is about the relationship between the individual self and the unity of self and other experienced in spiritual awakening.

Most psychologists claim that a healthy self is the goal of human maturity. Yet many of the Asian spiritual teachings say that there is no self. They teach that the sense of self is delusory and that belief in the self is the greatest obstacle to spiritual progress. For contemporary seekers, who for the most part are pragmatic and just want to "get on with it," this conflict of ideas is often a source of doubt and confusion. They ask: If I am to be more aware of my feelings and needs, as Western psychology advises, if I am to think for myself and maintain my boundaries, how am I to achieve the cosmic unity and unconditional love promised in spiritual teachings? And if I am not truly a separate self, how should I reconcile myself to living in this separate shape? If the experience of my body is also delusory, what can I do about the sensations and hungers that I feel in my body?

As you will see, because of my own particular path to enlightenment, this book presents a somewhat different view than many other books on this subject. It does not emphasize changing one's beliefs or behavior, although that is certainly part of the enlightenment process. Instead, it describes how enlightenment—the experience of one's own nature as subtle, unified consciousness—is revealed through deeply inhabiting one's body. Through this internal contact with our body, we come alive within our own skin, at the same time that we experience ourselves as open and unified with everything around us. This means that our tangible sense of existing in our distinct form develops as we transcend our distinct form. Although it seems paradoxical, we become more present and authentic at the same time as we become more permeable and transparent.

I will begin by telling you briefly how I came to the understanding presented here. Like many stories of awakening, mine begins with a crisis, an injury that shattered the identity that I had created for myself. When I was ten, I became a dancer, performing with a dance company in New York City. I grew up in a strictly atheistic background, and dance was my spiritual nourishment. The discipline of a dancer's life has much in common with monastic life. The rigor and focus of the daily classes, of physical exercises done repetitively in unison with other dancers, can quiet the restless mind, and dedicate the heart to a single purpose. During performances, communion with the dark, responsive expanse of the audience can instill the awe of connecting with something greater than oneself. I had also felt, since early childhood, a numinous presence in nature and in the sky. Before performances I would pray to this presence. I felt that I could draw it inside my body, and that it would displace my fears or self-consciousness until there was nothing left but the dance itself.

When I was twenty-five, during a rehearsal, I injured my back so severely that I could barely move at all. After two years of trying a variety of healing methods, I had surgery on my spine that fused me in the injured, off-center position. I felt like I had been cut in half and glued back crookedly. I was disoriented both physically and mentally. All my ideas of myself as an artist, my carefully trained body, my visions of the future, were completely gone. I could no longer feel the numinous presence that I had known since childhood, but I lay on the floor of my dance studio and sent prayers into the void.

Gradually, I began to notice a strange sensation. I could feel currents, like waving blades of grass, coming up from the floor and moving through my body, pulling me toward alignment, with no effort on my part. I also found that I could see light around my body, and a luminous weblike structure in the air. I became curious and began to experiment. I found that if I attuned inwardly with a very subtle focus, some of the discomfort in my body would begin to ease. One night I had a dream that I was entering a dark stage and my whole body was made of light. Another night, I dreamt the words "God is consciousness." I had no idea what these dreams meant, but they caught my attention.

Since I was still teaching dance for a living, I began to teach this kind of self-attunement to my students. I also studied whatever I could about bodywork, psychology, and spiritual philosophy. I made several trips to India and met many teachers, all the time applying the practices I learned to my own healing and teaching them to the people who came to work with me. I trained as an Alexander teacher and then as a psychotherapist.

It became clear that to heal my body meant also healing my heart, and refining my mind. I found that I could release the tensions in my body if I attuned to myself on a level that was deeper, and subtler, than the injury. The attunement exercises that I had discovered in my dance studio continued to develop, in response to my needs and those of my students. As my healing process uncovered increasingly subtle levels of my body, I was able to gain an understanding about the relationship between the body and spiritual openness.

In the early eighties, I lived for about a year at a Zen monastery in upstate New York. I had a favorite bench that I often sat on, looking out at a circular meadow. One day, sitting on that bench, I suddenly felt that my own body and everything I was seeing and hearing was made of luminous space. It was something like the presence that I had drawn inside my body when I was a dancer, but more subtle. And it was everywhere, effortlessly, a single orb of radiant, transparent life. Since then, this realization has never left me. I have found ways to deepen it, to gradually become more open so that I embody it more fully.

In the following chapters I describe how our most fundamental dimension of consciousness is the basis of both our individual sense of self and the transcendence of our separateness. Our own being and our experience of cosmic unity develop not only at the same time, but also in the same way, through the realization of fundamental consciousness. This process involves a gradual transformation of our entire being, including our experience of embodiment, our psychological health, and our relationship with the world around us.

I call this dimension "fundamental consciousness" but it has many names in the spiritual literature of the world. Some Buddhist writers call it self-knowing awareness, or nonduality, or Buddha-nature. Some Hindu traditions know it as Brahman, or Advaita (the Sanskrit term for nonduality), or pure consciousness. In the West it has been called Godhead, and cosmic and unity consciousness. Although there are differences in the philosophical explanations of these terms, they all seek to describe the same experience of spaciousness, authenticity, and unity.

Fundamental consciousness is beyond our mental representations, psychological projections, images, and archetypes. It is deeper, and more subtle, than the physical and energetic levels of our being. Since fundamental consciousness is not a mental concept, and not an object of consciousness but consciousness itself, it is difficult to comprehend until one has experienced it. One image often used to convey the experience of fundamental consciousness is the mirror, because fundamental consciousness reflects everything it pervades, while remaining empty and unchanged itself. It is not transient like the inner and outer events it reflects. It holds steady like a mirror while each moment of sensation, emotion, thought, perception, and action occurs and vanishes in its reflection.

For this reason, fundamental consciousness is sometimes called "the witness." This term, although traditional, causes some spiritual students to create a rift between their awareness and other aspects of their being. But fundamental consciousness is realized with our whole being. It is as much the essence of our love and physical sensation as it is the essence of our awareness. With the realization of this subtle dimension, every aspect of ourselves becomes open to, and unified with, the world around us. It is important that we do not assume an observational stance toward our experience, in which our own responses to life become objectified as something separate from ourselves. In the dimension of fundamental consciousness, the experiencer does not disappear; rather, it becomes one with its experience. As fundamental consciousness, we become a unified, all-pervasive experiencer. This means that we let go of our grasp on our perceptions and responses, only to experience them more directly and vividly.

This book addresses a phase of personal growth that is often ignored in both psychological and spiritual literature: the gradual deepening of enlightenment, following the initial realization of fundamental consciousness. In this phase we learn to live in (or as) the empty, pervasive space of fundamental consciousness, in union with the environment and cosmos, while becoming integrated, alive and whole within the space of our own body. If we attempt to eradicate our internal experience of ourselves, we thwart our spiritual progress and deprive ourselves of the great pleasure of becoming whole.

In order to describe the relationship between the sense of self and spiritual enlightenment, it is important that these terms, as I am using them in this book, are clearly understood. In chapter 1, I present what I mean by enlightenment, and describe the experience of living in the dimension of fundamental consciousness. This is a radical shift from a fragmented perception of "I" and "other" to an experience of our inner and outer life occurring in a single, unbroken expanse. Barriers between our self and our experience that we may not even have known were there dissolve, and we find ourselves in immediate, vivid contact with life.

Chapter 2 presents five different interpretations of the words self and selflessness that are often confused by spiritual students: the true, or essential self, the false self, ethical selflessness, logical selflessness, and ultimate selflessness. I describe what it feels like to become an essential self and how the qualities inherent in fundamental consciousness give us our authentic sense of self.

Chapter 3 is about the relationship of psychological healing to enlightenment. Meditation practices show that there is a potentially spontaneous process toward complete enlightenment. Just by sitting and doing nothing but breathing, the body and mind unwind toward the balance and openness of fundamental consciousness. In this chapter, I describe how this spontaneous process is impeded by the bound childhood pain and psychological defenses that we hold in our bodies, and how this binding can be released.

Chapter 4 is about the relationship of self and other in the dimension of fundamental consciousness. In our everyday interactions with people, the shift from self/object fragmentation to the oneness of enlightenment is a shift in our sense of boundaries. On one level, boundaries are a question of how much we give to others, how much we allow ourselves to receive from others, and what we consider intrusion or abuse. But there is a more subtle level of boundaries that can be described as the placement of our consciousness in relation to our body and the bodies of other people. As I will explain, most people create artificial boundaries to separate themselves from other people, or they attempt to live without boundaries, losing contact with their own body and self in order to connect with others. In fact, most of us manage to do both.

In the process of enlightenment, we realize that the fundamental dimension of our own being is continuous with the fundamental being of other people. There is no true barrier between us. At the same time, we begin to live in the core of our body and to relate to the world from this innermost core. The shift inward to our core is a deepened perspective on the world; it feels as if we are relating to people from further away. There is a sense that we are finding our true distance from other people as we discover our oneness with them.

In chapter 5, I show how the realization of fundamental consciousness transforms the body as well as our experience of embodiment. Our sense of identity shifts from the muscular surface of our body to the subtle, unified consciousness pervading our body. I describe how this shift affects our breath, the use of our senses, our physical comfort and health, and our relation to gravity.

Chapter 6 looks at the relationship between enlightenment, the experience of self/other oneness, and devotional, "I-Thou" types of spiritual experience. Events such as synchronicity and the effectiveness of prayer suggest a spiritual "Otherness" that responds to our needs and desires. In this chapter, I explore the mystery of this "Otherness." I speculate that it may be our underlying oneness with the vast dimension of fundamental consciousness that seems to inform and guide our progress toward enlightenment. An exchange, or dialogue between the incomplete self and the whole of fundamental consciousness can be consciously engaged in through communion with nature, visualization, and prayer. It can be experienced as a relationship with the cosmos, which matures and becomes more available to us as our realization of oneness matures.

The spiritual practices presented in this book grew out of the attunement exercises that I first discovered in my dance studio over thirty years ago. This method, now called Realization Process, is a series of gentle, precise attunement exercises to help people realize their authentic self and their oneness with other people, nature, and the cosmos.

Although enlightenment is a vivid, tangible experience of being alive, to describe it always sounds abstract, until you have experienced it yourself. I have included exercises from Realization Process throughout the book, so that the reader may better understand the experience I am trying to describe. But this is not a self-help book. The full benefit of the exercises requires the guidance of a qualified Realization Process teacher. I also describe the experiences of some of the people with whom I have worked. For the sake of their privacy, these descriptions are compounded of several different people and events, and all names are fictitious.

My intention in this book is to bring some clarity to understanding the process of becoming enlightened. Enlightenment is not something other than our humanness, it is the fruition of our humanness. It is also the innate potential of every human being, our birthright. In the following pages, I present the individuation of the self, the transcendence of the self, the transformation of the body, and the deepening capacity for relationship with other life as equally important, concurrent aspects of the realization of fundamental consciousness.

Although I have studied many different spiritual philosophies and disciplines, I am not aligned with any one school.

My main teacher has been the path itself: the unfolding of my own realization. The argument about what the experience of realization signifies about the nature of reality, and what truly constitutes enlightenment, is as vigorous in our society today as it was in ancient India. I believe that this is a valuable dialogue. We now have access to all of the world's wisdom on this subject, as well as to the contemporary Western knowledge of psychology. But most important, we have access to the mysterious, natural source of wisdom within our own being. If we examine our own spiritual development carefully, we may gain new insight into this advanced phase of human maturity.

1

Describing Enlightenment

Our own being, our own personal life, has hidden within it the transcendent unity of enlightenment. Most people live their whole lives without noticing this hidden potential, and both science and much of contemporary Western philosophy assure us that there can be no such innate or universal dimension of being. Yet many of us recognize its presence in moments of heightened attunement to ourselves or the world around us. This potential gives life a hidden meaning: the goal of knowing ourselves more deeply, of uncovering our true nature. Most of us create meaning in our lives by creating goals, such as family, wealth, artistic achievement. But the fundamental desire for enlightenment may cause us to feel unfulfilled, even after we have achieved our created goals.

In this book, as in many Asian spiritual teachings, enlightenment refers to a distinct and specific shift in the way you experience life. To understand the relationship of enlightenment and one's personal being, and how they both mature at the same time, we need to clearly understand the experiences that are meant by the words enlightenment and self. The following descriptions of enlightenment are based on my own experience, the experience of friends and students, and on the descriptions found in the spiritual texts of Buddhism and Hinduism. The point I wish to emphasize is that these accounts are not solely from my own experience, and are also not solely the paraphrasing of long-ago sages. Rather they are descriptions that many people agree upon, based on their own experience, that support the validity of the ancient texts.

THE REALIZATION OF FUNDAMENTAL CONSCIOUSNESS

Enlightenment is the realization, the lived experience, that unconditioned consciousness is our fundamental nature. It is the experience of our own being as a vast expanse of unbroken consciousness, pervading our body and our environment as a single whole. Our own body and everything around us appear to be made of clear, empty space, finer than air, at the same time that they appear substantial and solid.

The medieval Buddhist sage Longchen Rabjam (2001) wrote:

> Within the spacious expanse, the spacious expanse, the spacious vast expanse, I Longchen Rabjam, for whom the lucid expanse of being is infinite, experience everything as embraced within a blissful expanse, a single non-dual expanse (p. 79).

The ninth-century Hindu sage Shankara (1989) wrote:

> I am the supreme Brahman which is pure consciousness, always clearly manifest, unborn, one only, imperishable, unattached and all-pervading and non-dual (p. 111).

When people begin to realize fundamental consciousness, they report that they feel transparent, or permeable. They experience each moment inside of themselves and outside of themselves at the same time. One man told me excitedly that he had discovered that the world was round, because he could now experience the space behind him, and to the sides of him, rather than just in front of him. He had made a shift from a frontal self-object relationship with the world to an experience of continuity with the world. A woman told me that before realization, she felt that she was watching life; now she felt she was participating. She described her body as "clear-through open to life."

BECOMING AUTHENTIC

We do not create fundamental consciousness; we discover it as we relinquish our fantasies, projections, defenses, and fixed concepts. For this reason, as we achieve enlightenment, we feel that we are becoming increasingly real. We feel that we have discovered our true nature, and the true nature of the world around us. Enlightened experience is the opposite of abstract. It is not an idea about life, it is life itself.

Nondual Hindu philosophies claim that fundamental consciousness is the true nature of the universe—that it is actually the basis of every cell of our body and every atom of the universe. Nondual Buddhist philosophies describe the vast space of fundamental consciousness as the true nature of the mind, or "natural mind" or sometimes "primordial awareness." They often stop short of claiming that consciousness is a metaphysical reality, describing it instead as a refined experience of one's own mind, or as unobstructed openness to the flow of experience. However, some Buddhist teachers say that "the true nature of the world is the true nature of the mind" (Rabjam, 1998, p. xvii).

As we realize fundamental consciousness, we gain the clearest and least contrived experience that we can have of ourselves and our environment. This does not necessarily mean that our interpretations of events will be correct, or that there is any absolute truth as to how events should be interpreted. Rather, our perceptions, and our experience of our thoughts, emotions, and sensations become clear, as if they emerged directly out of the clear space of fundamental consciousness. Instead of diminishing the impact of experience through patterns of defense or fantasy, we can allow life to happen just as it is.

We have the sense that we are finally becoming who we really are; not something new, but something we have always been but only barely known. This is the true, whole "I" that has been hidden behind the partial, abstract "I"s that we usually mistake for our identity. Because of our innate true nature, we also possess the innate ability to recognize reality. Our lives are guided by our ability to tell truth from deception, balance from disharmony. As we realize fundamental consciousness, we recognize that our underlying reality has been the goal of our lifelong navigation toward balance and harmony.

Enlightenment is an experience unlike any other we have had because there is no duality in it. We do not have an experience of fundamental consciousness. Although the limits of language make it necessary for us to use the preposition "of," fundamental consciousness is actually realizing itself. It is self-reflecting. Longchen Rabjam calls it "self-knowing awareness."

Enlightenment is the phase of human development in which the mind comes to know itself.

The state of unity within our individual self and between our self and our environment is our most normal state. Several people have expressed fear to me about who they will become if they allow themselves to become enlightened. But once they have realized fundamental consciousness, they see that they have only become themselves, an intimately familiar and instantly recognizable being.

SOME MISCONCEPTIONS ABOUT ENLIGHTENMENT

Enlightenment is much easier to experience than most people think. Sometimes people become angry because I am asking them to experience what the revered masters have experienced, as if the attempt were futile, or even sacrilegious. Enlightenment is a relative term. The Zen master Maezumi Roshi once told me, "Enlightenment is easy to achieve. But to realize it completely can take many lifetimes." In this way it is something like being pregnant. You can be a little bit pregnant and no one would say that you are not "really" pregnant, but you have not yet come to full term. There is a tremendous range between the advanced enlightenment of the masters and the bit of enlightenment that can be easily achieved. When we first become enlightened, we have begun a phase of maturity that potentially stretches far ahead of us. But the beginning of enlightenment, as well as its progressive deepening, is accessible to anyone who is interested in it.

There is also a tendency for us to impose the sense of sanctity that some of us were taught in the Judeo-Christian tradition onto the principles of enlightenment. Much of Western religion teaches an attitude of reverence and humility toward a distant god, an image of patriarchal authority that we can petition but never truly know. Religious students are treated as children who can sit in the protective, vigilant presence of God, but have only the responsibility of obedience. In the more ritualistic forms of Asian religion as well, there is a hushed, hallowed quality when discussing the ultimate, and certainly there is great respect shown for the spiritual masters.

But the more advanced the teaching, and the students, become, the more the ultimate is presented as something belonging to us, as a wonderful but entirely natural part of our own nature. This part of ourselves can be neither taken away nor given to us by any external authority. I have found that many people who are ready for enlightenment are not achieving it because they assume it is some far-distant exalted state. The work that so many of us have been doing to become more real, more open to life, has been leading toward the realization of our fundamental dimension of consciousness. It is crucial to our personal growth that we recognize our essential reality and demystify our understanding of enlightenment.

Recently it has become popular to think of enlightenment as something that happens to us "by grace." This teaching goes along with the view that we cannot work to make enlightenment happen, we can only wait for it. As I said above, fundamental consciousness is not something we create, it appears spontaneously as we reach a particular degree of sensitivity and depth of inward contact with ourselves. However, there is much that we can do to increase our sensitivity and depth of contact. The received nature of fundamental consciousness does not mean that it is separate from our own nature, from the core of our own being. After all, we receive every part of our anatomy, as well as our capacity to feel, think, and sense.

From the perspective of most Asian teachings, grace is always happening. If we wish for something wholeheartedly, it begins to come our way. It is not bequeathed to us by a deity, with a mind and will of its own. We need to open to grace, just as we need to open to fundamental consciousness, in order to receive it.

There is also a popular teaching that we can reach enlightenment by simply accepting life as it is, in the present moment. Although this acceptance of life is helpful, even necessary, for the openness of enlightenment, for most people it is not sufficient for uncovering the subtle, pervasive expanse of fundamental consciousness. As I will explain more fully in the following chapter, there are unconscious bindings in our body, energy, and mind that limit our reception of the present moment, regardless of how attentive and accepting we are. In Zen Buddhism, they say that enlightenment is our "ordinary mind" clearly experienced. But there is a distinctive difference between our ordinary mind before and after enlightenment. When we are enlightened, our consciousness pervades our own body and everything around us. This is a more subtle dimension of consciousness than the usual condition of our ordinary mind. Another common misconception about enlightenment is that it is an "altered" state of consciousness. Enlightenment is often confused with the peak experiences that many people have, for example, while looking up at the stars, or witnessing the birth of a baby. But a peak experience is by definition a momentary event, often accompanied by intense emotions such as awe or ecstasy. Enlightenment is not a momentary alteration of consciousness that one goes to and returns from. For this same reason it also differs from the state of being hypnotized, and the trance state. Enlightenment is a clear, alert, but very subtle perception of the present moment based on a lasting refinement of consciousness.

Some people do have their first entry into enlightenment as a peak experience, a kensho or satori, in which they are dazzled by the sudden shift into the unity of fundamental consciousness. And some have had sudden deepenings of enlightenment as well, in which they abruptly experience much more of the space of fundamental consciousness than before. But enlightenment itself is not a temporary, nor a particularly charged emotional state. It is a lasting transformation of our being, involving our ongoing experience of life.

Sometimes enlightenment is said to be instantaneous because there is a definitive difference between being in the dimension of fundamental consciousness, and not being in it. Some people notice this difference suddenly, while others, once they do notice it, feel that they have been there for a while without registering or naming it. One may lose the realization of fundamental consciousness and get it back several times before it becomes stable. But once we do become stable in our realization, we continue to live there, while our realization very gradually deepens and expands. This means that our experience of fundamental consciousness gradually pervades more of our body, increasing our sense of internal depth and openness, and our sense of oneness with our environment.

In Zen Buddhism, the gradual process of enlightenment is said to consist of three thresholds. The first is an initial entrance into one's self-nature. The second is the longest phase.

Contemporary Zen master Sheng-yen writes, "The second threshold is in fact many thresholds...This is like a mountain range with ever-ascending peaks, which you must pass, one by one. The peaks are your own obstructions and vexations. This stage takes a long time, but with every peak crossed, your strength grows." The third threshold is a "final liberation from the wheel of samsara—the temporal realms of past, present and future" (In Loori, 2002, pp. 123–24).

One point that sometimes causes confusion about the gradual, relative nature of enlightenment is that Buddhist teachers make a distinction between what they call the gradual or progressive path and the direct or sudden path. These terms refer to the methods used to attain the initial realization of fundamental consciousness, and not to the subsequent process of deepening one's realization. The method offered in Realization Process is a direct path because it aims to evoke an immediate experience of fundamental consciousness. Gradual paths work with ritual and visualization techniques, cultivating concentration, dedication, discipline, and virtuous behavior as preparatory conditions for enlightenment. A direct path aims to evoke an immediate experience of fundamental consciousness. But a direct or sudden path does not mean that we become completely enlightened all at once.

Sometimes people ask why we have to work to achieve the realization of a dimension that is naturally part of ourselves. The Buddha taught that we are already enlightened, we are just not aware of it. But why not? Zen Buddhism speaks of our "beginningless greed, anger and ignorance" that separate us from the recognition of our true nature. Hinduism points to an accumulation over many lifetimes of confusion and attachments that pull us outward from our true self and obscure the basic purity of our consciousness. This explanation also puts the beginning of our trouble in the unfathomable past. And the Bible offers its own allegory of our fall from grace in the garden. One thing is clear. We are not born enlightened. Children, although undefended, are not experiencing the whole of the dimension of fundamental consciousness. There is a vast difference between the openness and unguarded love of an infant and the far-reaching clarity and intense but detached love of a spiritual master. As adults we must grow toward enlightenment as well as release the psychological defenses that impede this growth.

The last misconception about enlightenment that I will mention is that we do not know when we are enlightened—since there is no duality in the experience, we cannot experience it. This may be satisfying logically, but it is not the case. As I have said, fundamental consciousness is self-reflecting. When we become enlightened, we experience ourselves as empty space pervading both our individual form and everything outside of our individual form, as a unity. We experience both the stillness of pervasive space, and the movement of our perceptions, thoughts, emotions, and sensations, at the same time. We can say that fundamental consciousness is doing the experiencing, but fundamental consciousness is our own nature, our own being. Even though we experience ourselves as consciousness itself, we are still there, experiencing. Enlightenment is the most intimate contact that we can have with our own experience.

It is important that we do not make an object of fundamental consciousness, that we do not reify it into a thing in itself. Enlightenment is not a fixed focus on either the emptiness of pervasive space, or on the constantly changing "content" of the space. It is an opening up to the experience of both. In our ongoing experience of life, we are not holding an enlightened "state" but rather experiencing life in a spontaneous and vivid way. Any fixation on a particular focus or idea impedes the openness of enlightenment. But the shift from a fragmented self/object experience to the oneness of enlightenment is unmistakable. If this shift were not discernible, we would not know about enlightenment, yet the Asian spiritual literature is full of references to it.

UNITY

To become enlightened is to move from a fragmented experience of life to a unified experience. An ancient Buddhist text says, "The mind of the buddhas is all-pervasive. The mind of sentient beings is in fragments. To develop a scope like the sky has great benefit" (quoted in Rangdrol, 1993, p. 101).

Before we become enlightened our focus shifts from self to object, or from one modality of experience to another. We may experience another person quite fully but be only barely aware of our self. In another moment we know our own feelings, but our perception of the outside world is diminished. Or we may know our thoughts but not be conscious of our feelings, or sensation.

When we become enlightened we feel a continuity, a wholeness, of inner and outer experience, without any shifting of focus. This means that there is no longer any divisive schism between subject and object. We also experience our whole internal being at once, so there is no schism between thought, feeling, and sensation. All of these experiences are a unified whole; they occur in the single unbounded space of fundamental consciousness.

As I will explain in the next chapter and in chapter 4, the oneness of "I" and "other" does not negate the integrity of the individual wholeness of each person. The unity of enlightenment is not a merging of self and other, not a collapsing of our internal experience in favor of the environment. It is a continuity of the internal space of our own form with the internal space of the other forms around us.

DIRECT EXPERIENCE

To become enlightened is to experience life directly, without the interference of psychological defenses, projections, and preconceptions. As fundamental consciousness, we pervade both the subject and the object of experience. We become the unity of the perceiver and the perceived. We thus experience no barrier, no gap, between our self and our experience. We have the sense that all of our perceptions, thoughts, emotions, and physical sensations are arising directly out of the empty expanse of fundamental consciousness,

This experience is sometimes described with phrases like "thoughts without a thinker." It is easy to see how this description, if misunderstood, could produce more fragmentation between ourselves and our experience, rather than unity. The perceiver is not "gone" in direct perception, not pushed out of the way or ignored. Rather, the perceiver has become one with perception; has become the all-pervasive ground out of which perceptions arise.

When we realize fundamental consciousness, we begin to truly see, truly touch, truly hear. We move from imagination to actuality. For example, a woman who had begun to experience fundamental consciousness told me one day, in tears, that she had been seeing her life "through a filter." She had suddenly caught a glimpse of herself in the mirror and realized that she had not been seeing herself as she really is. She had either super-imposed on the mirror's reflection an image based on a fashion magazine ideal, or she had seen herself as her feared, negative image of herself, misshapen and homely. She had been afraid to see herself directly, without the filter. She also recognized that she was not seeing her husband clearly, or the other important people in her life. She was afraid that if she saw them directly, she would either see that they did not really love her, or she would see something that she did not like, and reject them.

This "filter" is actually typical of the human condition, but not many people ever notice the filter. There is a famous Zen story that addresses this same theme. A monk and his teacher are walking in the teacher's garden. The monk asks his teacher to explain a quote from the fourth-century teacher, Seng Chao, "The whole universe is of one and the same root as my own self." The teacher points to a flower and says, "Most people see this flower as if they were in a dream." The dream the teacher refers to is the cloudiness of our mind that separates us from our direct experience of life.

Before we are enlightened, we live abstractly, in our idea of life. Instead of seeing this particular flower, we see a general flower, like an image from a file in our mind marked "flower." And our "flower file" may be full of memories and associations that cause us to respond to the flower with feelings that are not directly related to this particular flower. In other words, we respond in a distorted or diminished way to our distorted or diminished perception of the world. We live, to some extent, as an imaginary character in an imagined world. Whether this fantasy is a romance or a horror story, it is not as satisfying as the direct experience of life.

Many people fear that if they awaken from their abstract dream-life, the world will be dull and ugly. But our senses, when (relatively) unfettered by psychological defense and distortion, reveal a more vivid, more luminous world than we have ever imagined. If we are seeing a preconceived flower, a composite of many past flowers, we will not notice the richness of color, softness of texture, the exact form of the present flower. We will certainly not see the subtle radiance that emanates from the flower that matches the light of our own aliveness. We will not notice that the flower is pervaded by the same radiant emptiness that pervades our own body, or that we are inseparably unified with the flower in all-pervasive consciousness.

In enlightenment, our senses become unified. We experience life as patterns of energy, as translucent, vibrant forms, moving through a vast expanse of luminous stillness. These energetic patterns are registered by all of our senses at once. We have a single, unified impression of life that is seen, heard, touched (felt), smelled, tasted all at the same time. For example, when we perceive the aliveness inside a branch of a tree, we experience that we are "seeing-feeling-hearing" it. The poet Rainer Maria Rilke describes this unified perception when he thanks the mythic musician Orpheus for "creating a tree in the ear." Rilke's Orpheus is attuned to the subtle foundation of life in which the visible world is audible and the audible world is visible.

Here is an exercise to help you experience the fundamental dimension of consciousness. As with all of the exercises in this book, it should be regarded as a "stretch" for your consciousness. Just as you would not stretch your physical body by holding onto an extended position all the time, for that would create more tension, please do not try to hold on to this attunement once the exercise is over. With repeated practice, the exercise will help you relax in the pervasive space of fundamental consciousness as your natural way of being.

Exercise 1—Attunement to Fundamental Consciousness

Sit upright on a chair or cross-legged on a pillow.

Close your eyes. Focus on your breathing, noticing how your breath comes in and how it goes out.

Bring your inhale inward through your head, so that you make deep inward contact with yourself, and release the breath as you exhale.

Bring your attention down to your feet, and feel that you are inside your feet, that you inhabit your feet. Experience yourself inhabiting the internal space of your feet.

Feel that you are inside your ankles and lower legs, filling them with yourself. Experience yourself inhabiting the internal space of your ankles and lower legs.

Feel that you are inside your knees. Balance your awareness of the internal space of both knees. Find both those internal areas at exactly the same time. Feel the absolute stillness of the balanced mind. (Don't hold the mind still. The subtle mind is still because it is balanced.)

Feel that you are inside your thighs. Experience yourself inside your thighs.

Feel that you are inside your hip sockets. Balance your awareness of the internal space of your hip sockets; find them both at the same time. Feel the stillness of the balanced mind, and the movement of your breath at the same time. These are two different aspects of yourself: the mind is still and the breath is moving.

Feel that you are inside your pelvis. Attune to the quality of your gender inside your pelvis. This is a not an idea, but a qualitative experience: what your gender feels like to you. Bring your breath down into your pelvis, and feel it pass through the quality of your gender.

Feel that you are inside your midsection, between your pelvis and ribs. Attune to the quality of your power (your personal strength) inside your midsection. Bring your breath down into your midsection and feel it pass through the quality of power.

Feel that you are inside your chest. Attune to the quality of your love, inside your chest. Bring your breath down into your chest and feel it pass through the quality of love.

Feel that you are inside your shoulders. Experience yourself inside your shoulders.

Feel that you are inside your shoulder sockets. Balance your awareness of the internal space of your shoulder sockets; find them both at the same time. Feel the stillness of the balanced mind, and the breath passing through the stillness of your mind, without disturbing the stillness. Let your breath be so subtle (it feels like half-breath, half-mind) that it does not disturb the stillness of the mind.

Feel that you are inside your arms, wrists, and hands, all the way to the fingertips. Experience yourself inside your arms, wrists, and hands.

Feel that you are inside your neck. Attune to the quality of your voice, your potential to speak, inside your neck. Bring your breath down into your neck and feel it pass through the quality of your voice.

Experience that you are inside your head, and inside your whole face: inside your forehead, your eyes, your cheekbones and nose, your jaw, mouth, lips, and chin, and inside your ears.

Feel that you are inside your whole brain. Attune to the quality of your understanding, inside your whole brain. If you do not know what this means, try to remember a time when you were writing something, and waiting for the right word to come to mind. This may help you remember the quality, the feeling, of your intelligence or understanding. Bring your breath back through your head into your brain and feel it pass through the quality of understanding. Let your breath be subtle enough to pass through the internal space of your head and brain.

Now feel that you are inside your whole body all at once. If we say that the body is the temple, then you are sitting inside the temple, with no part of you left out.

Keep your breath smooth and even, as you inhabit your whole body.

Keeping your eyes closed, mentally find the space outside your body, the space in the room.

Experience that the space inside your body and outside your body is the same continuous field of space. Let it pervade you. Let your breath be so subtle that it moves through the space, on the inhale and the exhale, without disturbing the stillness of the space. Your body is still, the space that pervades your body is still—only the breath is moving.

Now open your eyes.

With your eyes open, feel that you are inside your whole body at once.

Mentally find the space outside your body.

Experience that the space inside and outside your body is the same continuous field of space. It pervades you. You are experiencing this present moment inside you and outside you, at the same time.

Experience that the space that pervades your body also pervades the objects around you, and the other people in the room. Everything and everyone is pervaded by the same space, the same subtle dimension of fundamental consciousness.

Experience that the space pervading your own body also pervades the walls of the room. Fundamental consciousness is so subtle that it even pervades the walls of the room.

Sit for a few minutes in the clear, pervasive space of fundamental consciousness. Breathe silently and smoothly. Let your thoughts, emotions, sensations and perceptions occur in the field of fundamental consciousness without disturbing or changing it in any way.

Sometimes when I teach this exercise, people ask me how large they should visualize the space outside of them. This is not a visualization exercise. The space of fundamental consciousness is really there. We are only realizing it. The space will be as large as you are capable of realizing it at this time. If you do not immediately experience the space inside and outside your body as one unified space, you will with repeated practice. The repeated intention to experience fundamental consciousness will finally evoke the new "wiring" needed for this subtle experience.

People also ask me what to do about distracting thoughts as they attune to fundamental consciousness. Our thoughts, feelings, sensations, and perceptions are the content of the clear space of fundamental consciousness. They do not affect fundamental consciousness. So you can let your thoughts, feelings, and sensations occur while remaining in the realization of fundamental consciousness. If you find that you become so focused on your thoughts that you lose the experience of fundamental consciousness, simply bring yourself back to that experience. There is nothing wrong or "not spiritual" about having thoughts, emotions, or sensations. Enlightenment does not mean having an unthinking mind, but rather a "non-abiding" mind, a mind that is not fixated on thoughts or feelings but allows them to occur unhindered. As you become stable in fundamental consciousness, all of the content of your consciousness will flow freely and vividly through you. The depth and clarity of our reception and response to life increases as we become enlightened because we are no longer trying to control or defend against our experience.

FUNDAMENTAL CONSCIOUSNESS IS UNCHANGING

The dimension of fundamental consciousness never changes. When we realize this most subtle aspect of ourselves, we experience a vast, unchanging stillness pervading our body and our environment. We feel that we ourselves are fundamentally timeless and changeless. Zen Buddhism expresses this with the phrase, "I have never moved from the beginning."

Yet the life that occurs within our fundamental consciousness is all movement and change. All the systems that make up our being, such as our blood, nerve impulses, our stream of mental associations, our meridians of subtle energy, as well as the flow of circumstances in our lives, are in constant motion. The more we experience the absolute stillness of fundamental consciousness, the more freely the movement of life takes place. We become healthier physically, we respond more deeply emotionally, and our thinking becomes clearer and more creative.

If you practice the exercise of attuning to fundamental consciousness, you may feel streamings of energy inside your body. Like fundamental consciousness, energy is an essential aspect of ourselves. The more open we are to life, the more energy we feel in our body.

Although energy is an essential aspect of our nature, it is not our primary dimension. Many people practicing spiritual and therapeutic disciplines experience energy in their body, or in the environment, before they realize fundamental consciousness. The shift into the experience of oneself as energy from the experience of oneself as only physical matter, or only mental concepts, is so radical and liberating that many people assume they have reached the ultimate dimension of existence. It is important for our continuing development that we understand that fundamental consciousness is our primary nature. Fundamental consciousness pervades the energy in our body. Another way of saying this is that energy currents and vibrations move through the stillness of fundamental consciousness, without disturbing the stillness. However, when we realize fundamental consciousness, we also experience a more subtle level of our energy system, a very subtle vibration that occurs in our whole body at once.

The cultivation of energy without the realization of fundamental consciousness can produce imbalance and discomfort. We may feel overwhelmed by our own energy, or by the energy around us in our environment. The realization of fundamental consciousness grounds us in our true self, as I will explain more fully in the next chapter, and centers us in the subtle, vertical core of our body. If we experience our own nature as the clear, unchanging stillness of fundamental consciousness, our energy can move freely through our stillness, without overwhelming us. One woman told me she no longer felt like a "walking whirlwind," manipulated and disoriented by powerful inner and outer currents.

There are techniques for protecting ourselves from unwanted influences in the energy dimension, but these involve holding an image of a surrounding light or some other protective boundary. These techniques diminish our direct experience of life because they involve a fixed use of the imagination, and they also promote an attitude of fearfulness. They are not necessary when we live in the dimension of fundamental consciousness.

For example, a woman came to see me who had lived in a spiritual community for many years. She had recently stopped her meditation practice because she had an experience that badly frightened her. She had felt such overpowering waves of love during her meditation that she was afraid she would go crazy if she allowed them to continue. When she learned how to attune to fundamental consciousness, she was able to let the waves of love pass through the unmoving space of her consciousness, without disturbing it. She experienced herself as steady and stable, and at the same time, she experienced the streaming energy of her open heart.

Once we are secure in our realization of fundamental consciousness, we can open without fear to our own energy and the energy in our environment. We become like an empty vessel. Whatever is in the vessel is temporary and does not alter the primary emptiness of our nature. No matter how powerful the movement of life becomes, it does not change the absolute stillness of fundamental consciousness.

This is the paradox of enlightenment. We are able to receive the stimulation of life even more fully than before we were enlightened. Because we have more access to the internal depths of our being, we feel everything—joy and pain—more deeply than before. But at the same time, we experience our being as whole and steady, as an unchanging ground of consciousness. One of my teachers once likened this state to the biblical burning bush. "We burn," he said, "but we are not consumed."

Both our physical and our emotional pain are secondary to our fundamental nature. No matter what we lose or suffer in our life, this core of our being, our true reality, cannot be damaged. It has not moved from the beginning, and it will never move. Thus, as we become enlightened, it is easier to be at peace with even the worst of our circumstances. We can allow ourselves to mourn or rage, to risk new relationships and situations, because we know that our fundamental nature will always survive. Here is an exercise for direct experience.

Exercise 2—Seeing and Hearing with Fundamental Consciousness

With your eyes closed, feel that you are inside your whole body at once. Now mentally find the space outside your body. Experience that the space outside and inside your body is the same continuous field of space, pervading you.

Keeping your eyes closed, let yourself hear the sounds around you. Make no effort to listen to them, but just allow them to occur in the space of fundamental consciousness. Experience that the sounds occur in the space without changing or disturbing the space. The sounds are movement, patterns of vibration, occurring in the motionless space of fundamental consciousness. Experience that the space itself is doing the hearing.

Now open your eyes, and again find the space that pervades you. Experience that the space that pervades your body also pervades the objects and the walls of the room.

With your eyes open, let yourself hear the sounds around you, without making any effort to listen to them. Now let yourself see whatever is in your field of vision, without any effort to look at it. Let the visual objects simply appear in the space of fundamental consciousness. Experience that the space is seeing, rather than your eyes. The eyes are just lenses; it is consciousness that sees.

Now let yourself see and hear at the same time, without any effort. The pervasive space of fundamental consciousness is seeing and hearing.

You can also practice the visual exercise with a moving object, such as a flickering candle flame, steam rising from a pot, or the leaves moving in the wind. Keep relaxing your focus so that your field of vision becomes one with the stillness of fundamental consciousness, while the visual stimulus moves through it. This can only be accomplished by relaxing your focus, not by forcibly holding your vision still.

Recently I was teaching this exercise in a beautiful country setting, overlooking the sea. We were standing by the sea, experiencing that the space of fundamental consciousness pervaded ourselves and the water at the same time, and allowing the space to do the seeing. One woman in the group expressed concern that the ocean would no longer look as beautiful if she did the exercise, because she would be looking through it rather than at it. She was making the common mistake of projecting her vision through the object, rather than relaxing her vision and seeing with fundamental consciousness. By the end of the week, she was amazed that the ocean looked more magnificent than she had ever seen it. She was experiencing it directly, without the filter of habit or defense. Fundamental consciousness pervades the object and reflects it without distortion.

The eyes are one of the most defended parts of the body, for almost everyone. In Realization Process, particular emphasis is put on relaxing the eyes and seeing with fundamental consciousness. If we do not relax our eyes, our habitual way of looking at the world will keep us in the fragmented condition of "I" and "other." In order to live in the unified dimension of fundamental consciousness, we need to allow the visual images around us to exist as they really are, without defending against them. To experience life directly, we need to receive the world, just as it is, in the empty, unobstructed field of fundamental consciousness.

SUMMARY

Enlightenment is the realization of one's own nature as the pervasive expanse of fundamental consciousness. It is a radical shift from the fragmentation of subject-object duality to the unity of our essential being. As fundamental consciousness, we experience ourselves as vast, clear, unbreakable, unbounded space, pervading both our body and our environment at the same time. We are all capable of realizing this subtle dimension, and our realization can continue to deepen and expand throughout our lifetime.

2

Self and Selflessness

Several years ago, I attended a discourse by a respected teacher of Asian religion. He spoke forcefully about how our true nature is selfless and empty. The atmosphere in the room grew bleak as we contemplated our true nonexistence and the nagging, persistent illusion of self in which we were all trapped. When it was over, a man behind me stood and asked the teacher how a psychotherapist, like himself, could help his clients overcome this illusion. The teacher answered that psychotherapy misleads people from the start by regarding them as human beings. "If you tell someone they are a human being," he said, "you are already reinforcing their illusion of self."

Enlightenment is often described as a state of selflessness. This description is not, as we shall see, untrue in every way. But it has led to confusion on the part of many spiritual seekers. Much of the confusion arises out of the misinterpretation of the words "self" and "selflessness" in the context of enlightenment. Selflessness is often misunderstood to mean a state of nonexistence, in which one ceases to experience oneself as a unique individual, or to experience oneself at all. Yet, paradoxically, the emptiness of enlightenment is also the emergence of our authentic being. It is the true nature of our humanness. Contemporary Zen philosopher Nishitani (1983), describing the field of emptiness, writes, "It is the field in which each and every thing—as an absolute center, possessed of an absolutely unique individuality—becomes manifest as it is in itself" (p. 164).

The teaching of selflessness is meant to help us let go of our defensive or manipulative grip on ourselves, to help us cease to create ourselves and cease to create the barrier between ourselves and our environment, so that we can receive our authentic existence. Nishitani writes, "Only when the self...stands on the ground of nihility is it able to achieve a subjectivity that can in no way be objectivized" (p. 16). And, "Through this negation the person is broken through from within and the personal self discloses itself as subjectivity in its elemental self, as truly absolute selfhood" (p. 72). This received sense or quality of existence is sometimes described as impersonal. Yet it is the core of our person. Whether we call it "clear light" or "bare awareness" as the Tibetan Buddhists do, or the "pure Self" as the Hindus do, or "elemental subjectivity," as Nishitani does, it is still the fundamental nature of our being.

The problem that often arises when selflessness or nonexistence is taught as an end in itself is that it persuades people to deny, or "block out," their experience of themselves. In its most radical form, it tells people that they are not really human beings. Hearing this, many people obediently make up their minds to ignore their desires, judgments, emotions, and talents—in short, to pretend that they don't exist. This self-limitation reinforces and builds on the limitations that all human beings have already imposed upon themselves since childhood. Instead of furthering enlightenment, it obstructs the inward attunement and self-knowledge that is required for the realization of spiritual unity.

We are all familiar with the stereotype of feigned piety in Western religious traditions. Often this sanctimonious, falsely smiling character has simply been convinced that nothing less than perfect goodness is acceptable to the Lord. In similar fashion, when spiritual students are taught that enlightenment is nonexistence, the result is too often a strangely vacant, diffuse, or emotionally flattened, unreal human being. The tragedy of this situation is that to limit our human reality is to limit our spiritual reality, for they are actually one and the same. Enlightenment is our humanness, fully realized.

In the Western psyche, the teaching of selflessness tends to evoke images of the self-denial and self-sacrifice of Christian saints. Most of us were taught as children not to be selfish. When we hear what sounds like the same message from authority figures such as spiritual teachers, it touches our distant memory of these early admonitions, and the fear of parental punishment. It may also touch a more subtle injunction that many of us received as children against being fully oneself—a separate person with volition, feelings, desires, and cognitions of one's own.

The residual shame and guilt of our childhood are compounded by our failures and our sense of inadequacy as adults. For many people, hearing or reading that they don't really exist, or should not exist if they want to be spiritual, causes them to work harder at self-effacement and at suppressing their personal qualities. It further diminishes their appreciation of themselves. The self-contact required for enlightenment, however, is based on self-acceptance. In order to free ourselves from the constrictions that obscure our true nature, we need to see through our self-loathing to our original innocence. We need to regard ourselves—even our anger, pretensions, and fears—with compassion and clear understanding rather than seeking the oblivion of nonexistence.

Nonexistence is a concept. We can understand it philosophically, but we cannot experience that we do not exist—that which is supposedly experiencing nonexistence is always still there, existing. We can experience ourselves as empty space, but that fundamental subjectivity is still there as empty space. To imagine that we do not exist may help us let go of our grip on ourselves, but it should not, in my view, be considered enlightenment itself. Enlightenment is the lived experience of the luminous transparency of our own being, and of all being.

The Tibetan Buddhist teacher Chogyam Trungpa Rinpoche (1988), wrote, "The whole idea is that we must drop all reference points, all concepts of what is or what should be. Then it is possible to experience the uniqueness and vividness of phenomena directly. There is tremendous room to experience things, to allow experience to occur and pass away. Movement happens within vast space" (p. 14).

The intellectual understanding of nonexistence can help us begin to let go of our habitual modes of perception. However, the release obtained in this way cannot affect the deep-rooted psychological holding patterns that constrict our being, particularly those patterns that have defended against painful emotion. And we will not find ourselves in vast space unless we realize fundamental consciousness throughout our whole being. Enlightenment is not just an open intellect, but also an open heart, and an open body.

Another problem with the teaching of nonexistence is that for some students, this concept becomes a fixation. They become entrenched in an abstract stance toward life, which obscures the openness and actuality of enlightened experience. The teaching of selflessness also causes many people to fear the possibility of enlightenment. Some writers have equated the fear of enlightenment with the fear of death. Dramatic language is often used to describe enlightenment, such as "annihilation" of the ego and the "great death."

There may be fear involved in releasing the psychological defenses that obscure our realization of fundamental consciousness, because they have given us a sense of safety and power. We may think that we will cease to exist without them. But we do not cease to exist. The process of releasing our defenses and opening to fundamental consciousness reaps an unmistakable deepening of all our human qualities, such as our ability to love, to think, and to experience pleasure. We have a felt sense of coming to life—of becoming fully born—within our body. An interesting paradox of the human growth process is that the barrier between our internal space and the space outside of ourselves dissolves as we fully inhabit the internal space of our body. Enlightenment is based on the internal awakening of our individual form.

As we become enlightened, we have a profound sense of being real, for the first time. Our previous existence seems shadowy and imaginary by comparison. In the dimension of fundamental consciousness, we experience our self as life itself, as existence itself. There is nothing abstract or impersonal about this feeling of life. For it is our own skin that awakens to touch, our own chest that softens and fills with love. It is literally that we have been numb, in our sensations, our heart, and our awareness, and now we are waking from that numbness.

The obstacles that arise for people engaged in this process are often related to a fear of life rather than a fear of death, a fear of becoming fully functional, and fully present. People sometimes worry that they will be "too much" for the people around them, or that they will be too conspicuous for safety. As young children we formed ourselves to fit in with our family, and this meant mirroring the particular limitations of our family members, and limiting our behavior and even our perception in response to our parents' approval and disapproval. All of us have had to make some compromises in the process of becoming an individual. To regain those diminished parts of ourselves as adults is to break the subtle taboos and betray the loyalties of our childhood.

For example, one woman told me that she would be "so powerful" if she allowed herself to experience her own strength that she would surely overwhelm, and alienate, everyone who met her. In our continued conversations, she related the power struggles she had fought with her father, and the awful moment when she saw fear in his eyes, when she realized that he was now on the defensive instead of her. She never allowed herself to feel any stronger than in that moment. And I remember another woman who wept when she first began to experience her own intelligence, mourning the loss of her mother who had withdrawn from her, hurt and bewildered, when she began to develop her own mind. And the middle-aged man who had been the youngest of five children and still maintained the tight, unbreathing stance of someone trying "not to make any more waves," as he put it, in a chaotic household.

As young children, the spontaneous self-love that springs from the enjoyment of our own senses and understanding often evokes pain or annoyance, even rage, in adults who have lost this self-love themselves. The sense of being separate, the privacy and psychological distance necessary to mature, is almost always intolerable to parents who themselves were not allowed psychological separation. Psychologists (Miller, 1981) have found that children will sacrifice these basic requirements of selfhood to maintain the warmth and nourishment of their parents' love.

There are also social obstacles to becoming more fully alive. Remember how only one little boy could tell that the emperor was naked? Our innate drive to think for ourselves and express our unique perspective on the world is hidden and forgotten for the sake of acceptance, for the comfort and safety of fitting in to our community. One man, as he began to experience the quality of his own being, asked, "Who will know me if I become myself?"

However, as the process of enlightenment progresses, these fears diminish. As we begin to embody ourselves, our felt sense of internal depth becomes the basis of self-possession and self-confidence. We are able to trust the validity of our experience, and to recognize its value. And this deepened self-contact is, at the same time, a deepened capacity for contact with all other life. It is not isolation, but an experience of basic connection and equality with other people.

When people continue to fear enlightenment, even as their realization progresses, it is usually because they are attempting to enlighten only a part of their being. Many spiritual teachings emphasize a particular focus for spiritual practice, either in the head, or the heart, or the pelvis. Also, if people are meditating without guidance, they may focus on the part of themselves that is most open and familiar to begin with. So, for example, they may awaken the spiritual dimension of awareness, without awakening the spiritual dimension of love or physical sensation, if they focus only on points in the head without focusing within the chest or pelvis. This may produce increasing fragmentation in their being, and result in feelings of vulnerability and disorientation. This partial realization, although it can result in extreme openness, cannot reach the fundamental dimension of consciousness, which is a dimension of wholeness. For this reason, it is very important that we attune to fundamental consciousness within the whole body.

Sometimes people use their involvement with spiritual life as a way of creating a more powerful persona. They use whatever energy or knowledge they've developed to artificially inflate their sense of self, and to project the impression of themselves as a superior being. At root, however, this narcissistic attitude is also a fear of truly existing—of being real. It is a strategy of compensation for a hollow, diminished experience of oneself. When we realize fundamental consciousness, we are capable of unguarded receptivity and fluid responsiveness to our environment. This is very different from the static, unresponsive attitude of the narcissist who attempts to push against, or blot out, the outside world.

To some extent, we all suffer from a narcissistic wound, from a deficit in our self-love and self-knowledge. Most people compensate for this deficit with artificial postures meant to create a stronger, more functional, and more lovable self. It is this "false self" that gradually dissolves as we become enlightened. As fundamental consciousness, we gradually dissolve the "bubble" of our self-protection. We dissolve our self-consciousness, our vigilance to our own behavior and the responses of others. Our sense of ourselves becomes an open, unbounded expanse of receptivity and responsiveness.

I will now examine five different interpretations of the words "self" and "selflessness" as they are used in spiritual teachings: the true, or essential self, the false self, ethical selflessness, logical selflessness, and ultimate selflessness. It is important for effective spiritual practice that we understand how these words apply to the experience of enlightenment.

THE ESSENTIAL SELF

Our true, or essential, sense of self matures with the realization of fundamental consciousness. We come to know ourselves as boundless, pervasive, pure consciousness. At the same time, we develop an experience of our individual being within this vast space. This is a felt sense of the internal depth of our own form, along with the movement of our thoughts, emotions, and physical sensations.

Our individual form is experienced as entirely permeable and transparent, unified with the world around us. But the unity of enlightenment is not a state of fusion. It does not mean that we lose our internal contact and become merged with the life around us. Although we can see and feel, to some extent, the internal life of the beings around us, we do not confuse our own self with them. Although we may have great empathy for other life, we cannot perceive the environment from someone else's perspective, or think their thoughts, or decide to move across the room in someone else's body. This is the mysterious paradox of enlightened experience: we become unified with our environment, and more fully our own unique self, at the same time.

I worked with a young artist who had a great resistance to experiencing fundamental consciousness pervading her. "I am already so open and vulnerable," she kept telling me. It was hard for her to believe that she would still feel intact as a separate person if she attuned to this core dimension of herself. Still, she persevered in the exercise (described in chapter 1) of finding the space inside and outside her body, and feeling that they are the same, continuous space. Then one night she had a dream that illustrated her growing realization. She dreamt that she was seated on a beautiful upholstered chair in the middle of an oblong room. She noticed that the room had no walls; it was completely open. But she felt secure, seated in her chair. As we attune to fundamental consciousness in our body, we gain the security of self-knowledge and self-possession, the ability to "sit" in our self, even as we become unbounded.

As fundamental consciousness, we pervade our own form as well as the other forms in the environment. This means that we are able to attune to the internal experience occurring in the life around us. Before we realize fundamental consciousness, we have to rely on facial expressions, gestures, and words to know what other people are feeling. Or, as some very sensitive people report, we feel the feelings of others in our own body, where it is difficult to tell if they are our own feelings or someone else's. But after our realization, we experience that our own consciousness is continuous with the fundamental consciousness of other people, animals, and plants. We can therefore focus within these forms to experience the qualities, and to some extent, the sensations and emotions occurring there.

We have direct, in-depth contact with other life, and we feel great kinship with other life, because the core dimension of our own being is the same as the core of other life. But our contact with other life occurs across space, from our own body to the body of another. If I feel someone else's grief, I know it is some-one else's because it occurs somewhere else in the field of fundamental consciousness than in my own body. I may respond to that person's grief with grief in my own body, as often happens because we are empathic creatures, but I will be aware then of the sequence of another's grief and then my own. This may seem obvious to some readers, but many people misinterpret the boundlessness of enlightenment as meaning that there is no felt distinction between one's own experience and another's.

As fundamental consciousness, we no longer sense our own subjectivity as walled-off from an objective reality "out there." We experience that there is just one consciousness reflecting both our internal and external perceptions as a whole. All life appears to arise from one unified ground of consciousness. Yet, our individual subjectivity continues to function. Our own unique responses, and those of other people, all appear to emerge out of the one open, mutual ground of consciousness.

Fundamental consciousness, pervading the whole internal space of our body, provides an experience of internal cohesion. For example, as fundamental consciousness, we can experience the internal space of our head and our legs at the same time. We can think, feel, and sense at the same time. This is the basis of true self-possession.

Our essential sense of self cannot be harmed or in any way affected by inner or outer stimuli. It is always unbroken and unchanging. So it is also the basis of a stable sense of safety in the world. Many sensitive people tend to "flee the body" when outside stimuli seem too abrasive for them. This is a kind of scattering of consciousness, a rapid, reflexive dissociation from themselves. For example, my student Anna was very reactive to loud sounds. Once, when we were working together in a quiet country setting, the neighborhood dogs began a spirited dialogue with one another from their respective yards. Each time a dog barked, Anna would lose track of what we were discussing. She realized that she went through life continuously distracted by cars, neighbors, sirens, and other sounds in her environment. After consistent practice of attuning to fundamental consciousness, she was able to allow the sounds to pass through the unchanging ground of her being without losing her concentration.

The scattering of consciousness occurs severely during trauma such as sexual or other forms of physical abuse. Recovery from sexual abuse is almost always a process of returning to inhabit the body after having dissociated from it. I worked with a woman named Penelope who was sexually abused by her father throughout her childhood. She was now forty, attractive, friendly, and successful in her work. But she could not be physically touched. If a friend casually put a hand on her shoulder or touched her hand, she would experience the same rapid scattering of consciousness that Anna felt in reaction to sounds.

Penelope worked through intense emotions of terror, rage, shame, and revulsion as she regained conscious access to the internal space of her body. She spent weeks trying to tolerate being in her ankles, expressing the fury and urgency to kick that she felt when she was inside them. It was a full year before she could inhabit her sexual organs and feel safe. Penelope and I worked directly on her aversion to touch. She would practice remaining inside her wrist and hand, and experiencing the quality of her essential self in her wrist and hand, as I held my hand several inches above hers. Gradually she was able to maintain her realization of fundamental consciousness throughout her body, as I put my hand on her wrist. It is also deeply healing for people who have been physically or sexually abused to realize that the fundamental ground of their being has not been in any way harmed or altered by their attacker. This essence of ourselves has "never moved from the beginning." It is always within our reach.

Fundamental consciousness is experienced as the insubstantial transparency of empty space, and, at the same time, as the tangible quality of being, or presence. Anna had always avoided social situations, because she felt overwhelmed by the personalities of other people. But when she began to experience the subtle quality of her essential self, she no longer felt too fragile for contact with other people. This tangible sense of self also gave her a sense of self-value that sustained her even during conflicts with other people.

Some writers have described enlightenment as becoming nobody. There is a popular phrase that we must become "somebody before we can become nobody," that we must build up an ego and then dismantle it. But in my understanding, we become somebody and nobody at the same time. This is not a somebody in the abstract sense, such as an "important" person or a "good" person, nor is it an energetic inflation of oneself.

It is the actual (uncreated) presence of being. Emptiness and qualitative being are simultaneous attributes of the realization of fundamental consciousness.

Nondual Hindu philosophy claims that the "I" that we each experience as our own is the same "I" in all of us. Fundamental consciousness has an inherent quality of "I"ness, a quality of "I exist." Yet we each experience this "I" as emanating from our own individual form, as the center of our own individual locus of being. We are each the center, and, in a sense, the origin, or the wellspring, of the one "I" of fundamental consciousness. The more we mature in our enlightenment, the more we lay bare this innermost reality.

However, our essential self is not something other than our individual self, with its particular memories, talents, desires, and suffering. We cannot ignore ourselves and think that we will arrive at ultimate reality. We cannot "transcend" our suffering by ignoring it. When someone, for example, decides to "disidentify" with his grief, because he has been taught that suffering is "not really him," he will do this by fragmenting (dissociating) his awareness from his internal experience. This is accomplished through an actual holding of attention outward or upward, away from the movement of pain, or from the aching constriction within his chest. This action actually prevents his grief from discharging out of his body. By masking his inward experience, it also further obscures his realization of fundamental consciousness. Our essential self is a dimension of wholeness. If we fragment our being, we move way from the oneness of enlightenment.

Hindu philosophy uses the word Atman for the essential self. The Hindu scholar Chandradhar Sharma (1987) writes, "We have seen that the same reality is called from the subjective side as Atman and from the objective side as Brahman. The two terms are synonymous. The Absolute of the Upanishads manifests itself as the subject as well as the object and transcends them both" (p. 25).

Fundamental consciousness is realized through inward attunement to the internal space of the body, and in particular, to the subtle channel that runs through the vertical core of the body. This means that realization is based on inward penetration to the center of our individual being. The subtle channel is called *sushumna* in Hindu yoga, and the central channel in Tibetan Buddhism.

Most people live their whole lives without any contact with the vertical core of their own body. This is because our access to the core is obstructed by psychological defenses—repressed memories and emotions that become embedded in the tissues of our body, making them too dense and rigid to be easily penetrated by our consciousness. One of my more humorous students told me, after his first experience of being in the vertical core of his body, "I've been most places in the world, but I've never been here before." Also, we each have easier access to some parts of the vertical core than to other parts of it, depending on our particular pattern of psychological defense. I will explain this more fully in the next chapter.

For each of us, the subtle channel in the vertical core of our body is our entranceway into fundamental consciousness. That is, when we access this core, we discover the subtle emptiness or transparency of our being. We know when we enter the vertical core of the body, for it has a specific quality. It has a fine, electrical charge, and within that, stillness and a quality that we can recognize as truth, or essence.

In my experience, practitioners who attune to their consciousness only in the space around them, without experiencing that their consciousness pervades the subtle core of their body, do not enter into the qualitative being aspect of fundamental consciousness. And although they may achieve an immediacy of perception, they do not experience unified consciousness pervading their perceptions. For this we need to contact and let go of ourselves from the subtle core of the body.

Here is an exercise to help you attune to the subtle channel in the vertical core of your body.

Exercise 3—Finding the Subtle Core of the Body

We can enter the subtle channel anywhere along it. In Realization Process, we enter through three main points: the center of the head, the heart center, and the pelvic center. Do not strain to do this breathing exercise; follow the instructions as well as you can without effort. We begin by finding the center of the head.

Sit upright on a chair, or cross-legged on a pillow, and close your eyes.

Mentally find the center of your head.

This is an area between your ears and between your face and the back of your head, the center of the internal space of your head. (I do not mean the center of the forehead, or the crown chakra on the top of the head.) Most of us live a little above and in front of the center of the head. If you are in the center of your head, and not above it, you will feel a resonance down through the whole vertical core of your body, just by being in the center of your head.

Feel that the center of your head is in the center of the all-pervasive space of fundamental consciousness.

Inhale through your nostrils and bring the breath into the center of your head. Then exhale through your nostrils.

Let the breath be smooth and subtle, and direct it into the center of your head. If you have difficulty bringing breath into your head, begin by imagining the path of the breath. When this becomes easy for you, integrate the breath with the image.

Now initiate the breath from within the center of your head. Let the center of the head draw in the breath. Exhale by releasing the breath from within the center of your head. This is an internal breath, as if you were breathing air that is already inside the center of your head. It should be a very subtle breath, as if you were breathing a combination of breath and mind, or as if the mind were breathing inside the center of your head.

Find a point in the center of your chest, as inward toward your spine as you can focus. This is the heart center (or heart chakra in the Hindu yoga system).

Feel that the heart center is in the center of the all-pervasive space of fundamental consciousness.

Initiate your inhale from within your heart center. The heart center draws in the breath. Again, this is an internal breath, and there should be a subtle "mental" quality to the breath. Exhale by releasing the breath from within the heart center.

Next, find the center of your pelvis, an inch or two below your navel and as inward in your body as you can penetrate with your focus.

Feel that the pelvis center is in the center of the all-pervasive space of fundamental consciousness.

Initiate your inhale from within your pelvis center, as you did in the other two centers. Exhale by releasing the breath from within the pelvis center.

Find all three centers (of your head, chest, and pelvis) at the same time. Feel that the breath initiates from within all three centers at the same time. It can take some practice to be able to breathe within all three centers. Keep the breath going in the center of your head, and add in the other two as you can. Exhale by releasing the breath from within the centers.

Feel that the whole vertical core is in the center of pervasive space, inhaling and exhaling.

Staying in all three points, open your eyes. Take a few breaths from all three points with your eyes open. Let yourself feel that you are in the center of all-pervasive space. Instead of experiencing the room from the surface of your body, you are experiencing it from the subtle core of your body. This may feel like a deepened perspective on the room.

Fundamental consciousness is not blank space; it is not a lifeless void. It is the ground of our human experience. The Zen philosopher Hisamatsu writes, "But the nothingness of Zen is by no means something unconscious and unalive as is emptiness. Rather, it is the subject that knows itself clearly and distinctly. For this reason, it is also called 'heart,' 'self,' or 'the true human being'" (quoted in Stambaugh, 1999, p. 78).

As the ground of all our experience, fundamental consciousness contains all the essential qualities of our being. The vertical core of the body, as the entranceway into fundamental consciousness, is also the source of our essential qualities. Hindu yoga divides the vertical core's spectrum of qualities into seven main qualities associated with the seven main points along the core, called chakras. (The chakras are sensitive points along the vertical core where it is easiest to access the core.) Because the vertical core is a spectrum or continuum of qualities, it can be divided in any way. But any division is only schematic, for the purpose of understanding and cultivating the entire spectrum.

In Realization Process I divide the vertical core into three qualities: awareness, emotion (or love), and physical sensation. Physical sensation is attuned to through the bottom third of the vertical core, emotion through the middle third of the core, and awareness through the upper third of the core.

These three qualities are experienced as aspects of the ground of our being, aspects of the stillness that pervades all of the movement of life. Within this unchanging ground of awareness, emotion, and physical sensation, specific awarenesses, emotions, and sensations begin and end.

We can experience each of the qualities of awareness, emotion, and sensation pervading our entire body and our environment. Together, they make up the qualitative "feel" of our essential being. This is difficult to visualize or to grasp conceptually, but it is not difficult to experience. Each of the three qualities can be focused on separately, as you will see in the following exercise, but they are actually inseparable.

Depending upon our particular design of psychological defense and conditioning, we are each more open and more habituated to living in some of these qualities than others. The following exercise will help you recognize how you have been accustomed to experiencing life, and help you attune to the qualities that have been less accessible for you. You will get the best results from this exercise if you do not question intellectually what is meant by these qualities. Most people find that they can experience at least some of the qualities, if they don't stop themselves.

Exercise 4—Qualities of Fundamental Consciousness

Sit upright on a chair or cross-legged on a pillow. Your eyes can be open or closed.

Begin by repeating the end of the first exercise from chapter 1: Feel that you are inside your whole body all at once. Mentally find the space outside your body. Experience that the space inside and outside your body is the same, continuous space; it pervades you.

Attune to the quality of awareness. This means to become aware of being aware. You will find that you attune to the quality of awareness through the upper third of the vertical core of your body.

Experience that the quality of awareness pervades your whole body.

Experience that the quality of awareness pervades your whole body and your environment at the same time.

Attune to the quality of emotion. The quality of emotion is attuned to through the middle third of the vertical core. In its most refined state (that is, when we are most open to it), the quality of emotion is experienced as pure love, or bliss.

Experience that the quality of emotion pervades your whole body.

Experience that the quality of emotion pervades your body and your environment at the same time.

Attune to the quality of physical sensation. The quality of physical sensation is attuned to through the bottom third of your vertical core.

(If you have difficulty experiencing physical sensation, try looking at an object near you and seeing its texture. Living in the quality of physical sensation brings texture to our experience of the world. The quality of physical sensation is often not addressed in spiritual disciplines, but it is an essential aspect of our individual wholeness, our communion with other life, and our oneness with our environment.)

Experience the quality of physical sensation pervading your whole body.

Experience the quality of physical sensation pervading your body and your environment at the same time.

Attune to the qualities of awareness and physical sensation at the same time, pervading your whole body and environment.

Now add in the quality of emotion, so that all three qualities are pervading your whole body and environment.

Sit for a moment in this rich field of fundamental awareness, emotion, and sensation, allowing your breath to glide through the space without disturbing or altering your attunement to it. As fundamental consciousness, you can experience unity with the fundamental awareness, love, and sensation of everyone and everything that you encounter.

You may remember that in Exercise 1, the instructions called for you to attune to the qualities of gender, power, love, voice, and understanding. When the awareness, emotion (or love), and physical sensation of fundamental consciousness pervade the human body, it becomes further delineated into those qualities.

The essential qualities of fundamental consciousness are the most subtle, unconstricted dimension of the qualities and functions that make up our ordinary human experience. By attuning to fundamental consciousness, we deepen our capacity for awareness, emotional responsiveness, and physical sensation. We all grow up more open, or less defended, in some of these qualities than others. For example, I worked with a young dancer named Bella who was only comfortable when she was moving. During our sessions, she would slide off the couch and hang over, stretching and flexing her muscles. She kept herself attuned to the physical sensation aspect of her being.

We discovered that Bella had been a particularly sensitive child, acutely aware of the emotions and needs of the people around her. She described her mother as loving but frantic, with a "high frequency" expression in her eyes that disturbed Bella greatly. Her mother also depended on Bella as her primary source of love, a role that Bella felt inadequate to fill.

When Bella attuned to the three qualities of fundamental consciousness, she was able to experience physical sensation very easily. Emotion was a little more difficult, but the quality of awareness felt threatening even to attempt. She realized that she kept herself in almost constant motion so that she would not experience awareness. When I moved to the other side of the room and averted my gaze, Bella finally felt safe enough to attune to the quality of awareness. She then recognized that her fear of awareness was a fear of becoming aware of other people's pain, and feeling responsible for alleviating their pain.

In contrast, Paul had the most difficulty attuning to physical sensation, while the quality of awareness was the easiest for him. He was a large, muscular man, but his demeanor was timid and extremely polite, as if he were trying not to offend me. Paul had grown up with a violent father who abused his wife, bragged about his affairs with other women, and dominated the family. When Paul attuned to physical sensation, he said he felt like his father and he was afraid that he would be capable of the same destructive power. It was only when Paul learned how to attune to sensation, love, and awareness at the same time that he could trust himself to enjoy his own sensuality and power.

When people experience their fundamental qualities for the first time, they begin to feel both trust and appreciation toward themselves. This deep contact with oneself is the basis of true self-esteem and, as such, it brings significant healing to psychological distress. When we truly know ourselves, we are able to trust ourselves with intimacy, material success, artistic expression, and the various responsibilities of mature life. Also, when we can feel that an essential aspect of our own being is love, our yearning for the love we did not receive from important people in our childhood becomes more tolerable. Love emanates from the subtle core of our body, even when we are alone.

In summary, fundamental consciousness is the essence of our individual being because:

1. It is discovered through deep inward contact with our individual body, and with the subtle core of our body.

2. It pervades our body and reflects our individual thoughts, emotions, and sensations.

3. It contains the essential qualities associated with our humanness.

THE FALSE SELF

The false self is an amalgam of images, concepts, defensive attitudes, and bound childhood pain that we may mistake for our identity. Rather than having a felt sense of our existence as described in the last section, we have an imagined idea of who we are. All of us, to some extent, are caught up in this "dream" of ourselves; to be entirely without self-images or defenses is an ideal, which we can approach.

The behaviors and attitudes of the false self were created to cope with painful or confusing aspects of the external world. They were designed to attract love and avoid pain in specific, repeated situations in our past. As children, we distort our true responses and needs in order to become the child that our parents will recognize and appreciate, and to protect ourselves from feeling abandoned, misunderstood, shamed, deprived, etc. Daniel N. Stern (1985) describes the forming of the false self as the "center of gravity shifting from inside to outside" (p. 209). As we will examine more closely in the next chapter, the false self does not develop in isolation. It is a distortion of the self in interaction with the environment—an entanglement of self and other.

The false self is a constriction of our whole being, including our mental and emotional functioning, and our physical body. This constriction creates gaps in our ability to experience life, which are "filled in" with false images, compensatory attitudes, and inaccurate beliefs about ourselves and our environment.

These false images, attitudes, and beliefs, although unconscious or barely conscious, influence all of our life choices. The bound emotional pain in our body also colors or "haunts" all of our experience. For example, someone who is repeatedly criticized as a child may close the tissues of his body around his feeling of shame, in order to keep from feeling it. He may then hold an image of himself as a worthless person, or a compensatory image of himself as a superior person, or both. He may form a rigid belief that if people get to know him, they will also be critical of him, and may then avoid close relationships with people. Or someone who felt abandoned as a child may close her heart around her grief and cover this feeling with an attitude of apathy, or of sentimentalized love for others which is not, and cannot be, actually felt in her heart. She may also carry a dimly conscious belief that life is inherently sad, and that one can never be truly loved. The human imagination provides a multitude of variations on the themes of defense, compensation, and belief.

The rigid distortions of the false self become, over time, static patterns of tension in the body that literally trap us in their limiting patterns. They are densities in the tissues of our body. These densities obscure our realization of fundamental consciousness. They block our access to the vertical core of the body, and they obstruct our spontaneous, direct experience of life. They keep us reacting to the world as we reacted—out of what was then necessity—in our family of origin.

The various static attitudes and complexes of behavior that make up the false self have led some theorists to conclude that a person is made up of many different personalities. But it is really only the false self that is made of different personalities. The essential self that one discovers as fundamental consciousness is whole and unified.

The word "ego" is often used to denote the false self. The teaching of selflessness is then spoken of as an attempt to be egoless, and enlightenment is seen as the death of the ego. But the word ego is used in so many different ways that this teaching is also a source of confusion. For example, the word ego is sometimes used to mean self-love or conceit. But self-love can be false and compensatory, or it can be the healthy, spontaneous response to a felt sense of one's essential self. The conceit of the false self is a compensation for a lack of the self-love and self-enjoyment that we feel as our essential self.

The word "ego" is also used to mean the ability to organize one's environment, to navigate and discriminate, to make choices, to persevere toward specific goals, etc. Traditional psychologists point to these abilities as signs of what they call "ego strength." Many spiritual students are led to believe that the abilities associated with ego strength are in the way of their progress and need to be eliminated.

This confusion is further compounded by the fact that traditional psychology also views as ego strength the ability to defend oneself psychologically, and to create "psychic structures" by internalizing images of the external world. This topic will be taken up more fully in the next chapter. Here I will only say that a clear distinction must be made between the defensive activity of the wounded false self/ego and the self-confidence and volitional and cognitive abilities of the essential self, which continue to develop with spiritual growth. There is a vast difference between the skillful navigation of the essential self and the frightened manipulation of the false self.

It is the false self that gradually dissolves as we realize fundamental consciousness. As the densities of the false self are released, our body becomes increasingly permeable. What has seemed like our self has slowly vanished in the vast space pervading our body and environment.

If a rapid shift occurs from a defended stance to the permeability of the essential self, it can feel like a loss of self and may be frightening. However, it is most often a gradual change. The maturing individual has a chance to mourn the loss of old attachments and projections, and to appreciate the new directness of experience and the new type of substantiality that comes with the essential self.

As I have said, enlightenment is a relative term and a gradual process. This means that virtually everyone has some psychological entanglement and defense against life. A. H. Almaas (1986) writes, "The old idea is that the personality is the barrier and must be removed before there can be recognition of essential beingness. Our findings indicate that essence can be realized in steps, or in degrees, simultaneously with work on the personality" (p. 59).

It is crucial to our spiritual progress that we become aware of the remnant of childhood mentality in our behavior. If we know our own history of childhood pain, and how we tend to project it onto present situations, then we can gain flexibility in our behavior. Gradually we can release our childhood pain from its binding in our body, and see through the images and beliefs that are associated with this pain. But the first step is to become aware that it is there, so that we are not fooled by our own projections. For example, we may expect everyone in a position of authority to be dominating and potentially humiliating. If we do not become aware of the basis of this expectation, such as our early experience with a dominating, humiliating parent or teacher, we will approach all authority with an attitude of fear or anger. This attitude obscures our direct experience of the present-day situation. If we know about the relationship of our false self to authority, we may still feel fear or anger but we will know that this is not necessarily the appropriate response—not a true reading of the present situation—and we can choose not to act on it.

The false self is based primarily on the repressed or denied needs and emotions of our childhood. Therefore it is not helpful for our growth to further deny these needs and emotions in an effort to be "selfless." The false self is bound up in our mind, energy, and body. It does not go away when it is denied. Our innate drive for wholeness causes this bound part of ourselves to constantly seek expression in our behavior, dreams, illnesses, and even our life circumstances. Only our consciousness, our acknowledgment, of these parts of ourselves can free us from their spell. As we are able to witness these fragments of our childhood, our perspective deepens until finally we can access the vertical core of our body and the dimension of fundamental consciousness.

ETHICAL SELFLESSNESS

In the West, the teaching of selflessness often becomes equated with unselfishness. In general, Western religious teachings have emphasized ethical behavior rather than self-realization (enlightenment). The spiritual person is pictured as someone who always puts the needs of others before their own, who has no thought or concern for their own welfare. Our most respected spiritual figures have been people who exemplified ethical ideals, such as Mother Teresa.

The practice of selfless service to others is an important component of Asian religion as well. In Mahayana Buddhism, for example, the practitioner vows not to reach total enlightenment until all sentient beings have also reached it. This is the ultimate sacrifice, stretching over many lifetimes, but manifesting in the present as a commitment to furthering the enlightenment of others.

Ethical selflessness is a path toward enlightenment, but it is not enlightenment itself. Selfless service can help free the heart. Mother Teresa herself said that she engaged in service for the sake of her soul. Selfless service refers to a mode of behavior. Even the state of goodness, or the general attitude of benevolence, describes a person's intention to perform good and benevolent acts. It does not describe a person's experience of being. But enlightenment is an experience of being.

It is important to understand that the experience of our essential self does not diminish our capacity for selfless service. It does not make us selfish to attune inward to the core of our own being. In fact, the experience of our essential self facilitates unselfish behavior. This is because the essential self is relatively disentangled (psychologically) from the environment. The person who lives in fundamental consciousness makes fewer projections of childhood pain onto present circumstances. She or he is less likely to be motivated by unmet childhood needs for love and approval, and therefore has more freedom to be truly generous.

When we experience unity with other life, in the dimension of fundamental consciousness, we feel an inherent kinship with everything in nature. We are thus more likely to feel genuine concern for the people, animals, and vegetation in our environment. As our perspective deepens, we are more able to see the pain in the life around us, and we can also sometimes see the reasons for this pain. We then become better equipped to solve the problems in our society. There is also a subtler and more spontaneous level of ethical behavior experienced in the dimension of fundamental consciousness, but I will leave that subject for chapter 6.

LOGICAL SELFLESSNESS

Selflessness is often taught in Asian spiritual practices as the logical deconstruction of the existence of individual forms. This deconstruction is accomplished through an examination of the impermanence and interdependence of all phenomena. This approach says that all phenomena are "unreal" or without any "self-existence" because they are made of components, and are therefore subject to destruction and decay. All forms, including our own individual being, are unreal, in this sense, because they are impermanent. Phenomena are also said to be unreal and selfless because they are dependent upon other phenomena for their existence. They have no inherent existence of their own because they do not exist independently of other forms. For example, the table is made of wood, which comes from a tree, which comes from a seed, and so on, and therefore the table has no inherent existence of its own. In other words, there is no table essence that we can say is really a table.

A related philosophical approach claims that phenomena have no findable inherent existence, from their own side, because of the inescapably subjective nature of experience. Although we may all see something there beneath the silverware, we are all perceiving our own subjective version of the table. We are seeing our personal interpretation of the data conveyed to us by our own senses. We can each describe our experience of the table, but we cannot say for certain whether or not our experience means that there is really a table there.

Furthermore, the more closely (the more subtly) we regard the table, the more we find the luminosity and transparency of consciousness itself. Instead of the nature of table, we find the nature of the consciousness that perceives the table. The same is true when we look for our self. We do not find any thing—any object—that we can call our self. Instead we find the consciousness that searches for the self. The nature of the self is the nature of consciousness.

Like ethical selflessness, this abstract, logical understanding of selflessness can be a path toward enlightenment. It can help us loosen our defensive grip on our cognitive functioning, and on the objects of our perception. It can bring us finally to the nature of consciousness itself. However, as I said earlier, this teaching often holds people in an abstract stance toward experience, and in an ongoing activity of deconstruction, rather than the unguarded openness to experience that is enlightenment.

Ultimate Selflessness

The Asian teaching of reincarnation says that our individual personality persists from lifetime to lifetime as a subtle body, imprinted with our major memories, personal tendencies, desires, and attachments. These imprints produce life circumstances for their fulfillment or resolution. They can also be understood as densities or constrictions in our subtle body that obscure our realization of fundamental consciousness. In other words, they believe that our individual form exists because it is not yet fully realized, not yet fully pervaded with fundamental consciousness. According to this view, once we have attained complete enlightenment, we are no longer reborn. We have become entirely one with fundamental consciousness.

However, for the long duration of our process toward complete enlightenment, we do not lose our own locus of being, and our unique perspective in the unified field of fundamental consciousness. There is an inward center of reference, and a deepening essential sense of self. This essential experience of self is experienced as empty space, as the essential qualities of our being, and as the unchanging, unified ground through which our thoughts, emotions, sensations, and perceptions flow with increasing freedom.

It is important that we do not attempt to assume a state of ultimate selflessness, before we are actually fully realized, for this thwarts our progress toward complete enlightenment. The beginning of enlightenment is available to anyone who wants it. But, according to this view, complete enlightenment is a goal so far in the distance that it is really only a direction.

CONCLUSION

Fundamental consciousness is experienced as the basis of our essential sense of self, the "I am" at the core of our being. It is the Self, capital S, but it is discovered in each of us as the self, our own self. As we realize fundamental consciousness, we gain more sense of truly existing, even though the superficial signposts of our identity lose credibility for us. Before we realize our essential self, we often have difficulty knowing our own feelings and desires, and we can be easily manipulated and confused by the world around us. But when we experience our essential self, we have direct access to even our most subtle responses and needs.

Fundamental consciousness pervades our being and reflects, like a clear mirror, everything that occurs in us. This enables us to know our self intimately and specifically. Enlightenment is sometimes called selflessness because there is no image or concept of the self in it, but only the self itself. The essential self, as I have described in this chapter, is not vacant but vividly alive. It is impersonal only in the sense that it is universal, but it is personal in the sense that it is the essential nature of our individual, unique being.

As long as we are embodied and on Earth, we each have some imbalance, some incompleteness that has not yet spun out into fundamental consciousness. It is as if we are each coiled around our own point in fundamental consciousness.

Our unique design of defense and openness, what we have suffered and learned, our gifts and memories, give each of us a unique perspective on life, a unique way of experiencing life, and our own path toward complete enlightenment.

Exercise 5—Experiencing the Quality of Self

One of the ways that we can enter into the dimension of fundamental consciousness is by attuning to the quality of self within the body. Interestingly, this is a very particular quality, the same or nearly the same in all of us. The following is an exercise to help you experience the quality of self. If you do not think about what this means, but simply intend to attune to the quality, you will probably find that you can actually experience a particular quality that feels like self.

This exercise is almost the same sequence as Exercise 1 from the last chapter. Sit upright on a chair or cross-legged on a pillow. You can practice this exercise with your eyes open or closed.

Begin by breathing smoothly and evenly through your nostrils.

Bring your attention down to your feet. Feel that you inhabit your feet, that you are the internal space of your feet. Attune to the quality of self inside your feet.

Feel that you are inside your legs, that you are the internal space of your legs. Attune to the quality of self inside your legs.

Feel that you are inside your torso, including your pelvis, midsection, and chest. Feel that you are the internal space of your torso. Attune to the quality of self inside your torso.

Feel that you are inside your shoulders, arms, and hands, and that you are this internal space. Attune to the quality of self inside your shoulders, arms, and hands.

Feel that you are inside your neck. Attune to the quality of self inside your neck.

Feel that you are inside your head—your face and your brain. Attune to the quality of self inside your head.

Feel that you are inside your whole body all at once.

Attune to the quality of the pronoun "I" as deeply as you can in your body.

As that "I," allow yourself to let go of everything else. This "I" in the depths of your body is aware of your inner experience and the outer world, but it has no entanglement, no grasp on your inner or outer experience.

Mentally find the space outside of your body.

Experience that the space inside and outside your body is the same, continuous space.

Sometimes people ask me why I use the words "self" or "I" in this exercise, rather than words like "essence" or "being." I use the words "self" and "I" because I have found that they are most effective at helping people enter into the wholeness of the internal space of the body, and the experience of their fundamental nature. Although the words "being" and "essence" are often used to describe the idea of the essential self, they do not evoke the actual experience of it. The essential self feels like our self.

3
The Healing Process

Do away with your superimposition
carefully and with patience.

—Shankara

In the last two chapters I have said that we can realize a self-existent dimension of unified, fundamental consciousness, and that this realization is the basis of our essential sense of self or being. In this chapter, we will look at the relationship of psychological healing to the realization of fundamental consciousness. By psychological healing, I mean the recognition and release of painful memories and emotions that have become bound in the physical tissues of the body, along with the beliefs, projections, and defenses that result from these bound memories.

Although we can only guess at the nature of the infant's experience, it seems obvious that, compared to adults, infants are undefended, open to life, and must have some direct sense of themselves and the environment. It seems equally obvious that their experience is only the barest shadow of the realization of a spiritually mature adult. Infants do not have the self-knowledge, or the conscious access to the subtle core of their being, that is the basis of spiritual realization. The infant's budding sense of self and other is the rudimentary basis of the mature individual's experience of essential self and transcendent oneness.

Meditation practice reveals that the enlightenment process is as natural and spontaneous as a flower seed unfolding its completed form. Both Zen Buddhism and the Dzog-chen school of Tibetan Buddhism make it clear that one only needs to sit still and breathe in order to eventually become enlightened. However, our psychological binding in the body impedes the natural deepening of our breath and consciousness toward the vertical core of our body, and the realization of fundamental consciousness. As we release this binding, the spontaneous movement toward enlightenment is able to proceed.

How Emotional Pain Becomes Bound in the Body

People often ask why it is necessary to uncover their childhood pain, why it is not sufficient to change their current beliefs and behaviors in order to be happy. The binding of painful memories and emotions in the body is a binding of our instrument of experience, a contraction of our potential for awareness, emotion, and physical sensation. As long as our body, energy, and consciousness are bound up in the past, they are not available for present experience. We are unable to inhabit our body, to fully pervade our body as our essential self, as long as these contractions or densities of memory and emotional pain are held in our body. It is usually, although not always, necessary to know our childhood history in order to precisely contact and release our bound pain.

For example, a woman told me that whenever she tried to express herself publicly, she felt as if a demon were attacking her. She had a vague sense in her body of cringing away from this shadowy figure. In the course of our work together, carefully reviewing her memories of her childhood, she was finally able to see this demon clearly. She recognized the jealous rage in her mother's eyes and remembered the sickening, terrifying smell of whisky on her breath. She was then able to let her body move fully into the cringe, and to experience the childhood mentality that held her body in this defensive posture. By childhood mentality, I mean that she experienced herself as a young child, in the cringe. She experienced the consciousness, emotion, and physical movement of that terrifying memory while witnessing this younger part of herself with her present-day consciousness. When she did this, she was able, from her childhood mentality, to release her body out of the cringe, and to feel and finally discharge the bound terror from her body.

Usually the process of releasing a bound childhood memory occurs over time and requires repeated experiences of the contraction in the body, as well as a resolution of the childhood material. The woman just described had to come to terms with her mother's alcoholic fury, the nurturing she missed, and the decisions she made about her own incompetence, based on her mother's attacks. But just knowing the true identity of her demon, and recognizing that it belonged to her past, made her less susceptible to its influence. She was able to begin to express herself even before her cringing attitude and the terror resulting from the attacks on her were entirely released.

When we reconnect with a bound fragment of ourselves, the childhood mentality in the fragment is reunited with and expands our present-day consciousness. The released emotion frees and increases our energy system, and the released physical tension increases our physical comfort and health. We gain more of our unconditioned, essential being: more availability for awareness, emotional depth and physical sensation. We even look different. As I will describe in chapter 5, our body appears smoother and more unified as we release our psychological pain.

To the sensitive eye, we all look, to some extent, like Picasso's cubist portraits. The permeable field that is our consciousness, energy, and body contain hardened, static patterns in a complex composite of postures, expressions, and ages. For example, one pattern within this field may be a grief-stricken young child, another a stunned, overstimulated infant, a furious school-age child, and so on. In a normal conversation with an adult, these various fragments may all communicate their separate messages at once, in the rapid flickering of facial expression, vocal tone, emotional vibration, and physical attitude. The infant may communicate "please don't give me any more information, I can't take it," while the school-age child shuts me out with a defiant glare, and the grieving young child begs for love.

Some of the patterns in our field of being are simply lines of movement, well-traveled paths of response to painful circumstances that happened repeatedly in childhood and that are "triggered" by similar situations in the present. If these patterns are repeated often enough they begin to rigidify in the physical body. The physical tissues of the body harden along the lines of the repeated pattern. These patterns, as I have said, preserve the memory, the mentality of our age, and the emotion of our bound response to the painful circumstances. They also preserve the movement of our organism into the bound position. These patterns also rigidify in our body if they occur when we are very young (the younger we are, the more impressionable) or if our emotional response to a situation is extremely painful (if the trauma is severe).

The bound patterns in our body contain not only the painful moments of our childhood, but also defensive or compensatory attitudes that have been formed to protect us from further injury, such as the hypervigilant attitude of someone who was often abused, or the inflated, superior attitude of the narcissistic person who is compensating for the feelings of hurt and shame that he also holds in his body. Recently I worked with a woman who always kept a bright, uplifted expression on her face, no matter what she was saying. When I looked closely, I saw an edge of defiant bravery in this expression, and the sense of a young teenager. At the same time, there was a painful sadness in her chest and eyes, and the sense of a lonely, despairing child. Although she was able to feel these held postures easily when she attuned to herself, she had for years looked out at the world with these two static expressions, unaware of either of them. As she began to experience them more fully, she remembered feeling "darker and more complex" than her teenage peers, and making an effort to appear more upbeat in order to fit in with them.

It is not always necessary to uncover the exact circumstances that produced a static pattern in our body, as long as the pattern can be precisely contacted and experienced. An interesting example of this was the young man who came to work with me because he seemed unable to make money. He told me that his most important goal was to become financially secure, but he always sabotaged the advancement of his career. We worked for several months to uncover his negative associations with material wealth, but made little progress. Although he wanted very much to resolve this problem, he often seemed determined not to change. Then one day in our session he became conscious of himself in a posture that seemed familiar, and that I also recognized as one I had often seen him in. His gaze was downward and his chest deflated, and there was a kind of simplicity and serenity about him. Dwelling consciously in this posture, he said he felt like a devoted, humble Christian monk. Here was the fragment of this man that carefully avoided the temptation of material success. We never found out how he formed this attitude. Neither he nor his parents had been religious. It is possible that he mirrored the posture of his grandmother, a devout Catholic, whom he knew when he was very young. He believes that he formed his monk posture in past lifetimes. Whatever the truth of its origins, once he was able to consciously experience it, he was able to release it. In the process, he became interested in Christianity for a time, and finally rejected the pious ideal of poverty as inappropriate for the circumstances of his present life. At the same time, a subtle transformation occurred in his body. His upper chest expanded and filled with energy, dissolving the slight downward quality that had made him seem somewhat passive and withdrawn.

Our bound fragments of mentality, emotion, and physical body maintain their existence because they are cut off from our consciousness. They live in the past, until our present-day consciousness is literally reunited with them. It is not enough to know about our bound fragments. They must be experienced in order to be released. When our consciousness connects with the mentality of the fragment, it is no longer fragmented. When we can feel the old emotion in the fragment, we can finally discharge it. When our body returns to the contracted posture, we can access the old command to contract those muscles and relax them.

THE METAPHYSICS OF EMOTIONAL BINDING

The understanding that emotional pain is bound in the body has existed in the field of psychotherapy since its beginning. Sigmund Freud's student Wilhelm Reich (1945) made the phenomenon of body-mind connection the focus of his life's work. He became the first psychotherapist to write about a relationship between traumatic childhood memories (and the energy of their emotional content) and rigidities in the physical body. He called the rigidities "character armor," writing, "character armor and muscular armor are functionally identical" (p. 352).

Reich discovered a sensation of streaming in the body that he called orgone or vegetative energy. He felt that this energy was the fundamental stratum of life. (The physics of his day was also discovering the energetic stratum of the universe.) He wrote, "the orgone energy is bound in the chronic contraction of the muscles" (p. 372).

Reich claimed that there could be no psychological healing unless the emotional charge of the memories was liberated from the muscular armoring. He wrote, "I have also explained why remembering traumatic experiences is not essential for orgone therapy. It serves little purpose unless accompanied by the corresponding emotion. The emotion expressed in the movement (of release) is more than sufficient to make the patient's misfortunes comprehensible, quite apart from the fact that the remembrances emerge of themselves when the therapist works correctly" (p. 378). Reich then goes on to raise a fascinating question. He writes, "What remains puzzling is how unconscious memory functions can be dependent upon the conditions of plasmatic (cellular) excitation, how memories can be preserved, so to speak, in plasmatic awareness" (p. 378).

More than fifty years later, many schools of bodywork and psychotherapy have incorporated Reich's idea that painful memories are preserved in the body. Bioenergetics, coreenergetics, Ida Rolf's Structural Integration, A. H. Almaas's theory of "holes" in the body, Rebirthing, and Holotropic Breathwork, among others, have all reported a correlation between bodily tension and repressed memories, and the healing effect of releasing the emotional charge of the memories from the body.

But today it still remains a mystery how painful memories are preserved in the body and what exactly connects memory, energy, and the physical body. Although we need much more research into this subject, I believe we can approach an understanding if we include in our formulation an underlying, fundamental dimension of consciousness pervading the body.

An interesting question arises about the relationship between fundamental consciousness and our fragmented, bound consciousness. Asian spiritual literature says that fundamental consciousness is really our own ordinary mind, but clearly perceived. Fundamental consciousness is our mind, or our being, in its unbound, unmodified condition. Yet this same literature says that fundamental consciousness is never altered, has "never moved from the beginning." Then what is it that becomes contracted in our bound fragments and what is it that gradually realizes fundamental consciousness?

According to the Hindu teachings, there is a level of our consciousness that becomes fragmented (or imprinted) while fundamental consciousness does not. This has been called the causal level or buddhi. They speak of the buddhi as one of the "sheaths" of our being that obscure our true nature. The causal level of consciousness and fundamental consciousness are basically the same. It is only from the viewpoint of our constricted self that there is any kind of consciousness other than fundamental consciousness. However, we should not infer from this that the constricted self should be disregarded because it is "unreal." For, as we have seen, our own true body, energy and consciousness are bound in it. We must recover our bound self in order to become whole in the realization of fundamental consciousness.

The strange experience that occurs in enlightenment, in which the body feels like it is entirely open, or made of consciousness, seems to support the idea that consciousness is the primary level of the body. This suggests that there may be more going on in us than the "brain in the head directing the body" model has understood. One alternative possibility is that in every cell of the body, there is both consciousness and energy.

In my work, I call the binding, organizing level (or function) of consciousness the "movable mind." This refers to our ability to mold even the internal space of the body with our imagination. This aspect of consciousness seems intimately connected with the fascia that is everywhere in the body like an interconnected web. Reich believed that we create character armor in rings around the surface of our body. But we now know that this binding can occur anywhere within the internal space of the body, through the binding of the fascia and other physical tissues. Although it may produce an obvious postural change (such as stooping, or scoliosis), it is often a barely detectable density within the body. When we penetrate into the bound tissues with our focus, or through deep massage, we can experience the memory of ourselves in the moment of binding. For example, if we penetrate into the tension in our esophagus, we may experience ourselves as an angry one-year old trying to keep out unwanted food. This feels like a whole body, whole being memory of oneself as a one-year-old child in that situation.

Another important question is why some memories become bound in our body while others do not. Reich called the bound memories "pathogenic." Other writers have called them "unmetabolizable," using a digestive metaphor to describe this curious phenomenon in which some memories are literally stuck in our organism.

The newborn baby is relatively undefended. To be undefended means to be available for experience. We can therefore consider that the infant, within his or her limited sphere of budding perceptual and cognitive faculties, experiences the sensation, emotion, and awareness of each moment clearly and directly, without obstructing it. And although, as Daniel N. Stern's (1985) careful studies of infants have shown, they may know their own selves from the selves and objects around them, they nevertheless experience themselves and their environment without rigid, defensive fragmentation between self and other.

However, from birth, and probably from as early as the prenatal months and during the birth process itself, many events occur that cannot be tolerated by the undefended child. These are the events that have been called "unmetabolizable." They are either too painful, such as food or affection deprivation, too frightening, such as a loving face transforming into a grimace of anger, too stimulating, such as loud sounds, or, as the child becomes more cognizant, too confusing, as in being told that one is loved while actually feeling smothered or shamed. Many of the intolerable events of early childhood are quite subtle, such as one's gaze not being directly met, one's love not being clearly matched, or one's feelings or needs being misread, so that the child feels out of sync with his or her environment. A child's own responses to the environment may also be intolerable for the child, if they meet with disapproval, censure, or other negative emotional responses from his or her parents. It is easy to see that it is impossible to provide an entirely "metabolizable" environment for a child, no matter how loving and attentive a parent is.

The child recoils against these intolerable events and cannot be entirely available for them. It is in this withdrawing of availability, this protective diminishing of our experience and expression of ourselves, that we begin to bind our consciousness, energy, and body. In this way, the moments of our life that were too intolerable to experience fully are actually preserved in our consciousness, energy, and body.

Children unconsciously organize themselves in order to evoke the optimum love and approval from the people who are important to them. They may suppress their intelligence, for example, if their understanding of a family situation is denied; they may suppress their vitality if it is met with anxiety or envy. Children also unconsciously organize themselves to mirror their parents' design of openness and defense. If the parents are available for contact in the chest area, for example, but have suppressed their own intelligence, the child may adjust to the type of contact available. We are really like clay, sensitively molding ourselves in response to our environment. The only problem with this is that, if the same position is held over time, the clay will harden, and then our potential responsiveness is limited. As adults we are no longer entirely available for experience. There are unconscious constraints on our experience, where our awareness, emotion, and sensation are closed to life.

Here is an example of how this happens. An eighteen-month-old child is sitting in her high chair, being fed by her mother. She is not hungry and refuses the food, holding her mouth tightly shut to keep out the spoon. Her mother loses patience, becomes angry, and forces the spoon into the child's mouth while threatening the child with punishment if she does not eat.

In this event a combination of intrusive, angering, and frightening circumstances overwhelms the child. She tenses her lips, mouth, and esophagus as well as other parts of her body where she is experiencing anger, fear, and nausea. If this scene, or events like it, occurs repeatedly, this tension will become static and bound in her body. It will contain, for the rest of the person's life, unless some type of healing intervenes, the memory of the forced feeding, along with the anger, fear, and nausea she felt at the time.

The emotional content and the eighteen-month-old mentality bound in her body will color her future experience, particularly in "trigger" situations involving eating or taking in of nurture. The bound feelings and mentality will hang like a distorting veil, a "dream" between herself and her experience. Unaware of these memories and emotions influencing her experience, she may feel that life has an inexplicable undertone of scariness and intrusiveness. In circumstances where there is a possibility of nurture, she may respond with the same rage and fear of being overpowered that she felt as an eighteen-month-old child. She will also build a belief system and a complex of secondary defenses as a result of these unconscious influences. She may, for example, decide that she will never be nurtured in a way that meets her true needs and avoid intimacy, or that she is basically bad for causing her mother's anger (for having needs), or she may make an extreme effort to control her own intake of food, resulting in compulsive overeating or anorexia.

Most methods of psychotherapy treat only the secondary complex of beliefs and defenses. Many spiritual methods as well work only on changing beliefs. This method does provide some relief from psychological suffering. The limitation of this approach, however, is that we may make changes in our beliefs or behavior without releasing the childhood emotions and mentality bound in our body. We will then continue to be haunted by the painful events of our childhood, and our attunement to fundamental consciousness will still be blocked. We are held in a limited, fantasy-laden relationship with our environment to the degree that our childhood memories are bound in our body. But this is true of everyone, to some degree; it is the normal human condition. As we release this binding, our relationship with our environment changes. We awaken, little by little, from the dream of life to its actuality. We become free to respond to life from the depths of our being, and to receive life with vivid immediacy in the wide-open expanse of our consciousness.

RELEASING HOLDING PATTERNS FROM THE CAUSAL CONSCIOUSNESS

There are many ways to facilitate the release of our bound memories. Meditation techniques, particularly those that work with the subtle core of the body such as the core breath exercise in the last chapter, can help us let go of our defensive grip on ourselves. The core breath exercise works best if you follow it with a period of just sitting, without any particular focus of attention.

Fundamental consciousness is a disentangled, nongrasping dimension of our being. All of our experience moves through it without "sticking" anywhere. The subtle core of the body, and the points along it, are entranceways into this disentangled dimension. Therefore we can most easily let go of ourselves from this core. However, deeply entrenched defensive patterns will need more specific attunement to the psychological meaning and emotional content of the pattern, in order for us to let go of them.

Any bodywork method that penetrates into the physical or energetic levels of the binding or that helps people relax will also help the release of our holding patterns. I have found, though, that this release is often only temporary unless the consciousness within the binding is contacted. For example, people who receive very deep bodywork, such as Rolfing, often report that within a few months, the old tensions in their bodies have returned. This is because consciousness is basic to and organizes the energetic and physical levels of our being. For this reason, I have found self-attunement more effective than bodywork.

It is our childhood consciousness that organized the contraction of our energy and body. That same consciousness, if we can attune to it with our present-day consciousness, can let go of the contraction. Also, consciousness is fundamentally unbroken—it is the basis of our wholeness. When we contact the dimension of consciousness within our bound fragments, we contact our dimension of wholeness. This is the most direct, effective way of returning, or reconnecting, the bound fragments of ourselves to the wholeness of our consciousness. It heals our fragmentation at its root.

To contact the dimension of consciousness in our bound fragments, we need to penetrate not just deeply but also subtly into our binding, beyond the energetic and physical levels of the body. Here are two methods for achieving this subtle contact.

Exercise 6—Releasing the Bound Fragments

Mentally locate the center of your head, between your ears and between your face and the back of your head, as described in the last chapter. Feel that you are inside the center of your head.

From the center of your head, locate an area of tension in your body. By finding the tension from the center of your head, you are finding the core level, the level of consciousness, inside the tension. This subtle dimension within the tension will have the same subtle, mental quality as the center of your head.

Hold your focus steady within the area of tension, breathing smoothly and evenly through your nose (do not send your breath into the area). You may feel a subtle movement within the tension. It will feel as if your mind is moving within the tension. This subtle aspect of your being may move spontaneously toward release or toward the bound position, and then toward the release. Simply observe the movement, keeping your focus steady and subtle within the tension.

You can also facilitate the release by attuning directly to the emotional level of the binding. Keeping your focus subtle and steady within the area of binding, attune yourself to the emotional level of the tension. Keep breathing evenly. You may feel the emotion move within this area of your body. The release of the bound emotion can occur as tears, or more subtly as the movement of energy (emotion is energy). This emotional charge will dissipate as it moves out of your body. You may also be able to experience why you organized the holding pattern (what the binding is keeping you from experiencing or expressing). This will help you let go of it. You may also feel the quality of your childhood mentality; it will feel like the age that you were when you created the binding.

Not all tensions in the body are bound memories. Tension can be purely physical, caused by injury or structural imbalance. Physical tensions can also be released in this way, by contacting the dimension of consciousness inside the tension, from the center of your head.

Exercise 7—Releasing Bound Attitudes

This second method can be used once you have discovered a habitual or bound attitude in your body, such as cringing, defiance, hypervigilance, etc.

Let your body move into the bound attitude. Try to allow this movement to happen spontaneously as a subtle, internal movement rather than a volitional movement. If you can attune to the consciousness level of the holding pattern, it will feel as if your mind is moving into the attitude. Really experience yourself in this attitude. You may find that parts of your body that you did not know were involved in the attitude move into the pattern of tension. Because the whole body is interconnected through the causal consciousness, energy circuitry, and physical tissues, our bound patterns often involve a line of tension throughout our whole body. These lines of tension can even contract our bones.

When you can feel the whole pattern of tension, try to attune to the consciousness that is holding the tension. The same part of your childhood mind that organized the contraction in your body is still preserved in the contraction. Try to experience the childhood mind that is holding the attitude that you experience in your body. You may experience the age that you were when you first formed this pattern. You may also experience the emotional content of the pattern, and the memory of the circumstances that first evoked this attitude. As your body moves into the attitude, what is happening around you in your childhood environment; what is the attitude responding to, or what is it expressing?

As that childhood consciousness, you will be able to release the holding pattern, as simply as you can relax your hand after making a fist. You will also be able to feel and discharge the emotional content of the binding, if there is any. Again, the emotional release may occur as tears, or as the movement of energy through and out of your body. The emotion will have the quality of your age when it was bound in your body. For example, the rage of a two-year-old has a different quality than the rage of a six-year-old, or the rage of an adult. This is not a method of regression in the usual sense of experiencing oneself entirely as a child. Your present-day consciousness remains alert and witnesses the fragmented part of your consciousness, energy, and body that is bound in the childhood memory.

Once we are living in the dimension of fundamental consciousness, we can perceive our binding as densities in the empty, unified space of fundamental consciousness. Some people perceive it as areas of darkness, or numbness. It then becomes much easier to penetrate the contracted causal mind within these densities and reconnect it with the wholeness of fundamental consciousness. As the subtle structures or patterns gradually release, we experience the expanse of our consciousness as increasingly empty and unbroken.

Our fundamental dimension of consciousness, the core of our being, has never been injured. Even people who have sustained deep or very early childhood trauma, or who were born into an environment of pervasive, constant emotional pain can find this unified level of themselves and gradually reach a sense of well-being and cohesion.

A few years ago I worked with a woman who had endured such severe sexual abuse that she was unable to have an intimate relationship. She could not talk or think about the abuse without an overwhelming feeling of shame and nausea. She told me that she felt there was something essentially dark and "rotted out" about her, and she was sure that she could never rid herself of this feeling. But over a three-year period, she was gradually able to attune to the clear open space of fundamental consciousness pervading her body. She was then able to feel that even the rotted out sensation was simply lodged in the space like a veil, as were the terror and rage that she encountered in the process of getting well. As the years passed I watched her regain her essential qualities—courage and power in her belly, tenderness in her heart, and what she called "sweetness" in her skin and sexual organs. Finally she told me that she perceived the inside of her body as "made of light."

I am not saying that we no longer feel any emotional pain, as we release our holding patterns. It is our childhood pain, and its effect on our present-day experience that diminishes. In fact, as we release the bound energy of our past grief, anger, and fear, we gain emotional depth and fluidity in response to the current events in our life. We feel our emotions deeply, but we experience them as appropriate and as temporary, passing through the unchanging ground of our being.

We begin to experience life from one, unified perspective rather than from the many perspectives of our fragmented, bound consciousness. We grow toward wholeness. And we discover that our individual wholeness is, at the same time, the unity of self and other. This is the subject of the next chapter.

4
Distance and Intimacy

One of the biggest challenges on the spiritual path is to be able to get up from our meditation pillow and maintain our openness during the ordinary activities of daily life. Our fragmented, defended state was primarily created in relationships with other people, and so it is these encounters with other members of our own species that seem to be most rattling to our emerging sense of unity with the world around us. In order to stabilize in our realization of fundamental consciousness, it is important to understand how we can relate with other people while remaining in this open dimension of ourselves.

We will see in this chapter that we reach our greatest distance from other people, in terms of both our psychological and visual perspectives, as we achieve oneness with them. The poet Kabir said that detachment and love are the "twin streams of enlightenment." This means that individuation and transcendence, distance and intimacy, separation and oneness all occur at the same time as we realize fundamental consciousness.

THE SPATIAL NATURE OF PERSONAL GROWTH

Fundamental consciousness is experienced as the continuity,

the unity, of our self and the environment. As I explained in the last chapter, our realization of fundamental consciousness is diminished by rigid, defensive contractions in the consciousness, energetic, and physical levels of our being. These contractions fragment our experience of the basic unity of self and environment. In other words, when our realization of fundamental consciousness is obstructed (as it is to some extent in everyone), our experience of the self-environment unity is obstructed, because fundamental consciousness is the dimension of self-environment unity.

The limitation in our experience of the self-environment unity is a limitation in our sense of space. Instead of the spacious expanse of self-environment unity, our experience of space is contracted. In this contracted space, our perspective is literally shortened, so that people and objects seem closer to us in space than they actually are. Recently, when I was teaching this at a workshop, a woman told me, "All my life I've been saying I need space." This is a very common human complaint. Existential writers describing the human condition pointed repeatedly to this sense of suffocation and entrapment. To the extent that we are holding painful memories and emotions in our body, we live in a space that is too small for us. We cannot move or breathe or feel or think with ease. It is not the body itself that is a prison for the spirit, as some religious writing has suggested, but only the binding of pain in the body that confines us. As the causal level of consciousness releases its binding, we experience a sense of expansion and freedom.

In addition to shrinking the space we live in, so that we feel "glommed on" to the environment, our bound pain also creates a rigid fragmentation, or barrier, between the individual and the environment. In our defended body we feel separate from the environment. Wherever we have bound pain in our body there are gaps in our consciousness, gaps in our experience. We "fill in" these gaps with imaginary experience—the projections of our childhood fears, aversions, beliefs, and unfulfilled needs onto our present life. We experience a world "out there" of shadows and threats that is cut off from a world "inside" of fear and longing. This is the illusion of separateness that the Buddhists regard as our basic confusion.

We are thus both bound up with and divided from our environment. And the direction of growth is a simultaneous process of disentanglement and connection. Both disentanglement and oneness occur as we shift from living at the defensive boundary between ourselves and the environment, to living in the clear space of fundamental consciousness.

As I have said, to awaken to fundamental consciousness means that we have contacted ourselves inwardly to the subtle vertical core of our body. This is at once our greatest distance from other people and the basis of our experience of oneness with them. When we live at our defensive boundary, we communicate from our own surface to the surfaces of the people and things around us. For example, we experience our self in our face rather than in the center of our head, and we are aware only of the face of the person with whom we interact. When we touch, we feel only the contact of skin. But when we live in the vertical core and internal space of our body, we meet other life through the continuity of our own and the other's internal depth and content. We experience the qualitative being of the other person. For example, we can feel the quality of intelligence behind the face, the quality of love inside the chest.

This is more than connection—it is communion, the one-ness that is our true relationship with all other life. This communion occurs when we have grown further away from the world, inward to our deepest perspective in the core of our body. Our greatest contact with the world occurs across the unfolded distance, the true distance, of fundamental consciousness.

INDIVIDUATION

Many psychologists speak of the goal of personal growth as individuation. Margaret Mahler (1975) formulated a sequence of early childhood growth phases that became the basis of the predominant view of psychological development today. She said that as a newborn infant, one is in a psychological state of virtual fusion with one's mother and environment. One proceeds, given sufficient care and stimulation, to become increasingly aware of oneself and one's mother as separate entities. In the process, one passes through phases of symbiotic attachment to one's mother, a "practicing" phase of increased mobility and autonomy, a rapprochement phase in which one's focus shifts between attachment to one's mother and one's newfound autonomy, finally arriving at object constancy, at about age three. With the attainment of object constancy, one is able to be alone, apparently secure that one's mother will return eventually, and that one can enjoy oneself without fear of abandonment.

Mahler called this sequence the separation-individuation process. It has withstood the test of time because in clinical practice, psychotherapists see so many people who seem "stuck" at one or more of these phases before object constancy. It seems that we are all, to some extent, still struggling to achieve an individual identity, and to love others without loss of ourselves. By individual identity I mean the ability to perceive the world directly with our own senses, to understand our experience with our own mind, to feel that we inhabit our own body, to be able to surrender to the spontaneity of our own creativity and sexual passion, and to know that to a great extent, we can create the life circumstances of our own choice. In the therapeutic setting, we have come to recognize that the path toward this separate identity is fraught with taboos and obstacles of many kinds. It is a state of advanced psychological health and maturity. I can safely say that by age three, almost all of us have experienced some wound that will impede our progress toward this goal even as adults.

Mahler's theory of separation-individuation has been challenged and modified, most notably by Daniel N. Stern, and by therapists developing theories of feminine psychology. Stern's strongest objection to the separation-individuation theory is that it emphasizes the child's increasing separation and seems to ignore his growing capacity for intimacy. He writes, "Attachment and separation, or engagement and disengagement, are inextricably related, opposite sides of the same coin. . . . The structure and function of engagement and disengagement are interlocked so that the developmental history of one must encompass the developmental history of the other, regardless of which phase of development the child is in. The beginnings of separation and individuation must be contemporaneous with the beginnings of attachment" (1977, p. 128).

Stern's observations of infants have also led him to conclude that the infant never confuses himself with the environment; is never in a state of total fusion. He says that there is a "sense of emergent self from birth" (1985, p. 10). However, he does view childhood development as an increasing awareness of self and other, physically, emotionally, and verbally, which he calls an "acquisition of new senses of the self" (p. 11). Although he differs with the specific phases outlined by Mahler and feels she places too little emphasis on the child's growing connectedness with others, he does agree with her main thesis that the direction of human growth is toward increasing individuation, along with the capacity for intimacy.

The arguments of feminine psychology also center on the ignoring and implied undervaluing of the child's developing capacity for intimacy in Mahler's scheme. This apparent undervaluing is seen to result in an undervaluing of feminine behavior, which is typically more concerned with intimacy than separation. Carol Gilligan (1982) says, "Female identity formation takes place in a context of ongoing relationship since 'mothers tend to experience their daughters as more like, and continuous with, themselves.' Correspondingly, girls, in identifying themselves as female, experience themselves as like their mothers, thus fusing the experience of attachment with the process of identity formation. In contrast, 'mothers experience their sons as a male opposite,' and boys, in defining themselves as masculine, separate their mothers from themselves, thus curtailing their 'primary love and sense of empathic tie.' Consequently, male development entails a 'more emphatic individuation and a more defensive firming of experienced ego boundaries' " (pp. 7–8, quotes are from Chodorow, 1978, pp. 150, 166–67).

Feminine psychology argues that separation-individuation theory is gender-biased, judging psychological maturity by standards that do not encompass the developmental history of women. My own view of this subject is that, although men and women encounter different relationships with their mother and father, and different cultural expectations with regard to separation and attachment, both (undefended) individuation and the capacity for intimacy must be considered equally important goals of personal maturity for both genders. It is the legacy, passed from one generation to another, of bound pain and fragmentation, augmented by the shared imagery and beliefs of our society, that has created the frustrating, conflicted relationship between women who crave intimacy and men who opt for distance. For any individual to be relatively whole requires a balanced capacity for both oneness and separateness.

From birth, we are trying to become fully ourselves in the context of our love for our parents. If childhood development were solely a matter of separation, there would not be nearly the degree of conflict and pain, and binding of pain in our body, as there is in this delicate balancing act between our deepening self-awareness, and our intensifying love for our parents. It is almost always for love that we give up (bind) those parts of our self that do not meet our parents' acceptance. And it is almost always for the sake of autonomy that we close ourselves off from our parents' love, by closing our own heart, when that love does not include the recognition and sanction of our separate identity.

Mahler presents her separation-individuation sequence as the normal, natural phases of the developing infant and child. This implies that she believes, as I do, that there is a spontaneous unfolding toward individuation. However, I place individuation in the ranges of advanced personal maturity rather than at age three, as Mahler does. Daniel N. Stern (1985) voices a similar concern when he writes, "Clinical issues that have been viewed as the developmental tasks for specific epochs of infancy are seen here as issues for the lifespan rather than as developmental phases of life, operating at essentially the same levels at all points in development" (p. 10). Just as the child's capacity for love and for separation develop at the same time, the spiritually maturing adult discovers that unity with the cosmos and individuation develop simultaneously in the dimension of fundamental consciousness. The child's first inkling of intimacy and separation is the rudimentary form of the advanced spiritual master's oneness with others and internal wholeness.

For the adult, individuation is a progression from a state of being merged with other people to a state of increasing independence and capacity for love. The merged state is a dependence upon the responses of others in order to feel good, safe, strong, and complete. There is an inability to use one's own senses and understanding, or to perceive and think for oneself. There is a sense of never being truly alone with oneself, and not being able to experience one's own sensations, feelings and thoughts clearly. Stern writes that in situations of uncertainty, infants will " . . . look toward mother to read her face for its affective content, essentially to see what they should feel, to get a second appraisal to help resolve their uncertainty" (p. 132). This looking toward others to see what one should feel or think remains in the adult who has not yet discovered his or her separate identity.

R. D. Laing (1965) writes, "If the individual does not feel himself to be autonomous this means that he can experience neither his separateness from, nor his relatedness to, the other in the usual way. A lack of sense of autonomy implies that one feels one's being bound up in the other, or that the other is bound up in oneself, in a sense that transgresses the actual possibilities within the structure of human relatedness. It means that a feeling that one is in a position of ontological dependency on the other (i.e., dependent on the other for one's very being), is substituted for a sense of relatedness and attachment to him based on genuine mutuality" (pp. 52–53).

Some people defend against this incomplete, dependent feeling by withdrawing from contact with other people. They are afraid of being overwhelmed, or feeling consumed by others, because they have so little felt sense of their own existence. Others become "addicted" to love, searching desperately for anyone who will merge with them and help them feel alive.

RELATING IN FUNDAMENTAL CONSCIOUSNESS

In my work as a Realization Process teacher, I have discovered that the state of being bound up with other people can be observed in a person's placement of consciousness. I said earlier that before we realize fundamental consciousness, we relate to the surfaces of other life from the surface of ourselves. In fact, most people are not just on the surface of their body; they are in front of their body. By this I mean that they habitually relate to the world, and experience themselves, from the space in front of their body. When we live in the shortened space of the contracted self-environment unity, we experience the center of our being in front of our body rather than in the core of our body. To be bound up in other people is literally to live outside of our own body and self.

For reasons I will describe shortly, almost everyone has some degree of displacement of consciousness away from the vertical core and internal space of their body. Some people live just a little in front of their body, and others are much further separated from their true center. Some people relate by projecting themselves entirely into the person they are relating to, as if they were truly merged with them. I do not mean that they focus inside the other person's body, but that the locus of their being, where they experience the world from, is inside the other person's body. Much has been said about the subjective nature of our sense of time, how time sometimes seems slower or faster, depending upon our psychological state. In the sense that I am describing here, our experience of space, or distance, is also subjective and relative.

As I have said, when our psychological defenses hold us in the contracted self-environment unity, we feel both merged with and defended against the environment. When we contact another person from the space in front of our body rather than from the vertical core of our body, we are limited in our perception of that person and in our ability to interact. This is because the source of our awareness, love, power, and sexuality is in the core of our body. When our access to the core is blocked, we are less capable of truly perceiving or loving or of being sexually aroused by another person. Further, our interaction may be distorted by the childhood emotions and needs that are held in our body, that block our access to our core, and contract our experience of space. This means that we are not relating directly to the person we are with, but to earlier people and situations that the present relationship reminds us of.

Here are a few of the reasons that we live and relate to the world from the space in front of our body:

1. Shortened Perspective

Although a young child is relatively undefended, so that his experience of the self-environment unity is not defensively contracted, he still lives in a smaller experience of space than the undefended adult. Although the child's experience can only be a matter of speculation for us, we may rely on the assessment of expert observers like Mahler and Stern that the child begins life with only a rudimentary awareness of himself and the environment, and grows gradually toward individuation and relational ability. If you recall your own early childhood memories, you may notice that they take place in a small sphere of interaction; that the world consisted of the environs of a playpen, for example, or an object directly in front of you. But if you remember yourself as an adolescent, you may notice that your memory occurs within a larger context, such as a whole room. There appears to be a natural process of growth that expands our sense of space—our contact with both the internal space of our body and the external space of our environment—to the extent that it is not impeded by psychological defense. Although many young children have spiritual experiences, such as leaving their body or precognition, these are different than the experience of one's consciousness pervading and encompassing a vast expanse of space, extending in all directions, as occurs in spiritual maturity.

Our psychological defenses—the binding of consciousness in our body—occurred mainly in childhood, in interaction with the environment. Thus, these childhood defenses maintain the child's immature, up-close spatial relationship with the world in our adult body. When an adult relates to us from this shortened perspective, it is recognizably childlike. The person's lack of self-possession and lack of separateness from us makes that person seem dependent and malleable in the same way children are. Also, the parts of our causal consciousness that are bound in our defenses are not available for the process of maturation inward to the vertical core of our body. They remain held in the past.

2. Psychological Binding

The binding of childhood memory and pain in our body blocks our access to the vertical core of the body, and the realization of fundamental consciousness. The binding also prevents us from inhabiting the parts of our body where the memories and pain are held. We cannot inhabit the parts of our body that are bound. When we are unable to inhabit our body, our sense of self is displaced to the outside of our body.

3. Hypervigilance

As children, we manipulate our behavior in a variety of ways in order to maintain our parents' love. In this process, many of us become hypervigilant to the emotional climate and expectations of the environment. This is particularly so if our parents are violent, or unpredictably shifting in their approval and disapproval. Our attention shifts away from self-experience and becomes overly focused on the world outside of ourselves.

For example, I worked with a woman who kept her focus glued to my face during our sessions. The center of her being seemed to be just a few inches from my face, even though we were seated several feet from each other. When she began to experience her projected consciousness, she remembered a recurrent scene in her childhood. She was trying to play with her wooden blocks, as her mother rushed frantically around her, doing housework. When this woman accessed the part of her consciousness that belonged to herself as a young child, she was able to see her mother very clearly and could feel her mother's emotional pain. She associated this pain with the frequent conflicts between her parents that sometimes erupted into violence. She could also feel her own fear that if she "abandoned" her mother by concentrating on her blocks, something terrible might happen to her mother. Here we see how the maturity that Mahler called "object constancy" can be obstructed. This child was unable to be alone with her own activity because her mother's place in her life did not seem assured. As an adult she still "held on" to people with her eyes; she could not risk concentrating on her own inner experience.

4. Self-Objectification

We can add to this list the pressure of the mass media and social convention to conform our behavior and appearance to that of our peers, to live as a particular idea of a person rather than as our own self. Conforming to standard norms of physical beauty, material success, and moral choices diminishes our attunement to our own self, and unbalances our consciousness toward the outside world. This is noticeable, for example, in women who project and actually live in and relate from a static image of conventional beauty superimposed on their own face and body. Feeling themselves to be objects, they relate from a superficial, objectified position, cut off from subjective experience.

5. Learned Relational Style

One of the primary reasons that we relate to other people and experience our self from the space outside of our body is that we learned this relational style from our parents. Our parents are the first people we interact with in our lives, and our subsequent relationships are based on the relational style we learned from them. To the degree that our parents live in defended bodies themselves, they relate to us from outside of their bodies. We automatically match our parents' placement of consciousness in order to be in contact with them.

Parents who do not have much inward contact with themselves often give the young child subtle signs of disapproval as the child begins to achieve their own self-contact. These signs are often involuntary, unconscious facial expressions or, also unconscious, emotional vibrations of abandonment or anger. For example, a mother puts her two-year-old son on her lap as she always does, but this time the child looks at her from further back in himself, with a little more than his usual clarity. Responding only to what seems like a lack of closeness, the mother pulls the boy closer to her face and wraps him tightly in her arms. She wants to maintain the relational distance that feels comfortable and affectionate to her. However, this action actually impedes the new level of contact with her that the child is ready for. The parent may also convey a lack of recognition, as if the child has become a stranger, or a withdrawal of affection. The child receives the unspoken message that to relate in a way that does not mirror the parents' way of relating jeopardizes the bond of love between them. Many people I have worked with have reported some sort of familial taboo against this spatial/relational expression of individuation. Even though we actually experience greater contact with each other from the greater distance of our core, the shift into greater distance evokes a sense of risk.

For example, one woman was able to experience that she was relating to me from somewhere in the space between us, but she was reluctant to change it. After struggling with it for some time, she finally admitted to me that she did not think I really wanted her to make the shift inward. When I assured her that I did, her expression of disbelief quickly dissolved into tears. To shift her sense of self inward felt disloyal to her mother, with whom she had been very close. She felt that if she let go of her merged style of relating, her mother would be brokenhearted and might not even survive. She also feared being in the world without the superimposed projection of her relationship with her mother. She said that to be in the core of her body felt like "going it all alone."

Many people fear that they will lose contact with the outside world if they live in the core of themselves, or that they will be abandoned. They feel guilty for separating from the environment, or angrily defiant, as if the separation could only occur as an act of rebellion. Very often people tell me that it feels selfish to be in their core. Others are afraid that they will be more clearly seen and known by another person if they live in their core, and rejected for who they really are. Although I have seen these reactions numerous times, and experienced them myself, I am still amazed that to be inside one's own body and relate to the world from there can seem so fraught with danger.

I have often also observed the difficulty of separation from the parent's point of view. For many people, the enmeshed intimacy they enjoy with their young child satisfies the residual needs of their own childhood. Old rejections and losses are finally soothed by the dependent, clinging, unconditional affection of the young child. When the child begins to outgrow the parent's state of enmeshment, the parent feels abandoned.

I worked with a woman who felt loved for the first time in her life when her baby was born. She bloomed during the first two years of her child's life, becoming more content and confident than she had ever been. But one day she came to our session very upset. During their "cuddle time," which was her favorite part of the day, her daughter had refused to lie down next to her, preferring to play with her toys instead. When the woman insisted that the child lie down with her, the child threw a tantrum, and the mother became enraged and screamed at her. The mother was shocked and confused by the intensity of her own response. As she related the incident to me, she recognized that she felt like a hurt child herself when her source of love and attention was no longer focused solely on her.

As for her child, she learned that there was something bad about separating from her mother. She probably recognized that this event was in some way worse than those times she had been yelled at for spilling or breaking something. For besides the anger in her mother's voice and facial expression, there was also hurt, and the accusation of emotional betrayal. Many people find this taboo against separation at the root of their long-standing feelings of guilt. I don't mean to imply that one incident of this sort can cause a child damage. But if this difficulty with separation becomes a chronic element in the parent-child relationship, the child will grow up feeling that she is not allowed to exist as an individual.

When adults begin the process of accessing the subtle core of their body and relating to the world from their core, they often encounter, along with the childhood pain bound in their body, the taboo against growing inward and experiencing themselves as separate from their parents. Self-contact is a gradual process of resolving and releasing the pain of our early relationships. But almost everyone reports that they are able to love their parents more fully when they have gained some psychological distance from them, and given up their childhood wish for their parents to be different toward them. They are also more able to love the people in their present-day relationships, as they begin to connect with them across the true distance of fundamental consciousness.

Exercise 8—Relating from the Subtle Core

Here is an exercise to help two people relate to each other from the subtle, vertical core of the body, and experience each other in the expanse of fundamental consciousness. (For more relational exercises, please see my book, *Living Intimately* (Blackstone, 2002). The instructions are followed by both people at the same time.

Sit facing each other, with your backs upright.

Mentally find the center of your own head, between your ears and between your face and the back of your head.

Staying in the center of your head, look at your partner across the distance between you; be aware of the amount of spatial distance between you. Make eye contact with your partner across this distance.

Staying in the center of your head, mentally find the center of your partner's head. Do not leave the center of your own head, and do not project yourself into your partner's head. You do not need to move at all to contact the center of your partner's head from the center of your own head.

Now find your heart center, in the center of your chest, deep within the subtle core of your body.

Staying in your heart center, make eye contact with your partner across the spatial distance between you.

Staying in your own heart center, mentally find the heart center of your partner. Do not come out of your own heart center to connect with your partner, but subtly attune to your partner's heart center from your own.

Now find your pelvic center, an inch or two below your navel, in the subtle core of your body.

Staying in your pelvic center, make eye contact with your partner, still aware of the spatial distance between you.

Staying in your own pelvic center, mentally find the pelvic center of your partner.

Find all three points in your own body at the same time: your head, heart, and pelvic centers. Staying in all three centers, make eye contact with your partner across the distance between you. From all three centers in your own body, mentally find those three centers in your partner's body.

Feel that you are inside your whole body at once. Find the space outside your body, the space in the room. Experience that the space inside and outside your body is the same, continuous space; it pervades you.

Experience that the space that pervades you also pervades your partner. Let the space receive you both, just as you are in this moment.

When we find another person's core from our own, there is an unmistakable sense of contact between us. This contact feels like a perfect resonance, as if at root there were just one center, which we all experience as the center of our own body. It is the experience of oneness in the dimension of fundamental consciousness. One woman compared this experience to the "buzz" she felt when she was singing with someone and exactly matched their tone. We can experience this resonance with another person through the entire core of our body.

There is also, in this core-to-core contact, an automatic exchange of energy between people that we can feel occurring, and that can even be seen by a sensitive observer. On the level of the center of the head, the exchange feels like clarity, or intelligence. On the level of the heart, there is an exchange of love. Most people are surprised to discover that when they pull back into their own core, they experience a spontaneous exchange of love with another person. We are particularly used to going out of our body and self to express love, and to assure the other person that we love them. But this separation from our core actually diminishes our ability to love by cutting us off from the source of our love. On the level of the pelvic center, the exchange of energy has the quality of power, and sensuality. The spontaneous exchange of sensuality is part of our normal connection with all people, regardless of gender, and with all forms of life.

When I work with couples, I have them attune to each other in this way from all seven chakras as charted in the Hindu yoga system (the base of the spine, the sacral area, the navel area, the chest, the throat, the center of the head or center of the forehead, and the center of the top of the head) along the vertical core of the body. This deepens their contact with each other, and it also helps heal imbalances in their relationship, such as struggles over power and submission, or the giving and taking of love. A very common imbalance in intimate relationships is when one person is overly focused on the other, while the other person withdraws. When couples practice relating to each other from the vertical core of their bodies, communication, caring, power, and sexual exchange become deeper and more balanced.

Even in intimate sexual contact, the merging that occurs between spiritually mature individuals does not eradicate self-possession. We are unified with our sexual partner in the dimension of fundamental consciousness, and our energy systems do interpenetrate and blend. But we have our most intense, and most releasing, contact if we each remain in the vertical core of our own body. In this type of contact, both partners' centers are stimulated and opened. In this way, sexuality, or any exchange with another person, can facilitate personal, spiritual growth. When partners consistently practice this core-to-core contact, intimacy becomes a very effective spiritual path.

Exercise 8 is also an excellent diagnostic tool as well as treatment for many psychological problems, as it involves our ability to make contact with ourselves and our environment. Whatever wounding has occurred in our interaction with the environment since birth will be reflected in the limitations of our ability to relate core-to-core, across the actual distance between ourselves and other people.

When people are able to connect to the world from their own core, they feel less susceptible to rejection and abandonment. They have a felt sense that they exist, and will go on existing even if the person providing them with love and acknowledgment in that moment is no longer there. Virtually all of us had to negotiate an economy of love and autonomy in interaction with our parents. Thus, for most people, to experience self-possession and intimacy at the same time is a significant breakthrough. Many people have also said that as they experience other people from the core of their being, they are able to feel more appreciation and reverence for human life. The safety and spiritual connection that many of us experience in relation to nature can extend to our relationships with other human beings.

Understanding the spatial nature of personal growth gives us a new way to perceive and heal the boundary issues, and the dissociation from ourselves, that we suffer in our defended relationship with life. Even people with more severe so-called schizoid, borderline, and narcissistic problems, who have defended themselves by imagining the world to be all-me or all-other, can learn to integrate distance and intimacy when they experience the world from the vertical core of their body. As psychotherapists and spiritual teachers, we need to be able to recognize the shift in consciousness from the periphery of the body to the internal depth and core of the body that reflects the shift in perspective from entanglement and projection to individuation and connectedness.

We also need to be able to help people wrestle with the many taboos, familial and cultural, against continuing the inward path toward the realization of fundamental consciousness. Even if we are no longer in contact with our parents, the old threat of punishment for separation is still operative in our bound childhood mentality. And it is a terrible punishment that we imagine—estrangement, the cessation of love, the loss of belonging. Almost as potent is the fear of estrangement from our peers for separating from the conventional beliefs, behaviors, and goals of our social milieu. It takes courage to shift our loyalty from the conventions of tradition to our own judgment, which arises spontaneously in the dimension of fundamental consciousness.

We often experience a phase of painful aloneness as we separate psychologically from our family of origin and the standard imagery of our society. This phase is expressed in the philosophy of existentialism, in which the individual is seen as the sole point of reference. But this is an illusion; we are not alone. We exist in a unified field with all other life. The paradox is that the more we realize our individual existence, the more we experience that we are inextricably connected with the whole of life. We can relate to our community as caring and (relatively) free individuals, with the will and vision to work for change, as well as the detachment to live, without defensive boundaries, in the midst of the world's confusion.

DETACHMENT

As we shift from the contracted space of our psychological binding to the expanded, unified space of fundamental consciousness, we begin to experience detachment. Detachment does not mean a lack of responsiveness, interest, or passion. Rather, it is freedom from our entanglement with the world, from the projections of our past onto our present experience. It means that we have greater availability for present-day experience, greater depth and resilience in all the capacities of our being. We are able to be alone with our self, alone in our own body, and also alone with others, without the remembered voices of our early relationships.

Gradually we find that we can drop our agenda for getting our old needs satisfied, and our old wounds recompensed or avenged. We have less need for people to act toward us in a particular way, or to manipulate our circumstances through denial, clinging, avoidance, or aggression. We are more able to let life happen, without anxiety about the outcome of events. By detachment I mean this ability to allow ourselves and others to be just as we are, to let each moment of life—both our perceptions and responses—unfold spontaneously.

A few years ago I attended a lecture by a visiting Tibetan Buddhist teacher from Ladakh. A Buddhist teacher who lives here in the United States was translating for him, so they were sitting quite close to each other on the stage. I was struck by the relationship between these two men, but it took me a while to realize what seemed so unusual to me. Although there did not appear to be a particular friendship between them, there was also no defensiveness. They seemed to be receiving each other completely, without the usual guardedness, and without any trace of pulling back or pushing against each other. They were not trying to control each other, or themselves, or the audience. Although Tibetan culture is in many ways more formal than Western culture, more involved with protocol and hierarchy, these two spiritual teachers did not seem to be observing themselves, or presenting themselves to us in any fixed way. They appeared to be completely at ease and open to our appraisal. Their freedom gave the audience the freedom to respond honestly and spontaneously.

Detachment is the experience of flow, of allowing life to move and unfold without censure. Whatever happens within ourselves and our environment occurs without disturbing our attunement to the radiant stillness of fundamental consciousness. Even if we are profoundly moved by something, this response occurs as a transient feeling in the open expanse of our being.

Thus detachment does not at all mean that we become zombies, aloof from the emotional richness of human life. Detachment is the full, direct experience of life at the same time as we experience the unchanging ground that pervades our life. Just as we can hear music most clearly when we are silent, the dynamic interplay of our reception and responses to life is experienced most clearly in the stillness of fundamental consciousness. Although we will not act on all our responses, for our judgment is also functioning freely, we will experience the full range and depth of our sensations, emotions, cognitions, and perceptions without interference or distortion.

There is a Zen story on this theme about an accomplished Zen master whose wife has just died. One of the master's students is alarmed to find his great teacher, who has given such inspiring talks on the impermanence of life, sobbing in his garden. "Why are you crying?" the student asks. The master answers, "I am crying because I am sad."

Many spiritual students try to hold themselves in an attitude of detachment, when detachment is really a matter of letting life be just as it is. As I have said, our emotional responses gradually become less related to the projections of our childhood pain and more related to our present-day circumstances as we continue in our realization of fundamental consciousness. Although we do not become less passionate in our responses to life, our passion loses the urgency of our unfulfilled childhood needs to be loved, and becomes the free flowing of our love, sexuality, and intelligence in response to the life around us.

Exercise 9—Letting Life Go Through

Here is an exercise that I do with people to help them experience the unchanging, unbreakable nature of fundamental consciousness.

I ask the person to begin with the exercise from chapter 1: experience that you are inside your whole body at once. Mentally find the space outside your body, the space in the room. Now experience that the space inside and outside your body is the same, continuous space; it pervades you. Experience that the space pervading your body also pervades the other people and objects in the room. Experience that the space pervading your body also pervades the walls of the room. You are still in your body, as you experience this all-pervasive space.

I then tell the person that I have an imaginary red ball, about the size of a pea, and that I am going to gently toss the ball through the clear space of fundamental consciousness that pervades their body.

I toss the imaginary ball through the space over their right shoulder. Then over their left shoulder. Next, I toss the ball through the right side of their chest. Then through the left side of their chest. In this way, they can experience that even the substance of their body is permeable in the dimension of fundamental consciousness.

The tossing of the ball is not entirely imaginary because the movement of my hand creates a current of energy. Many people will flinch or subtly close their attunement to fundamental consciousness against this current. With practice, the person can remain open and allow the ball to pass through his or her body without flinching or closing.

This exercise can then be applied to daily life, allowing the various energies in the environment to pass through our attunement to fundamental consciousness, without our flinching, recoiling, or shutting out experience. This allows us to receive and respond to life fully while remaining grounded in our fundamental being. It allows each moment to register and transpire within the field of fundamental consciousness, without distortion. It also enables us to be in the presence of other people's pain and confusion without feeling threatened or overwhelmed.

In another version of this exercise, I stand close to the person and create an emotional energy in the field of fundamental consciousness, such as anger or sadness, by making a sound that expresses that emotion. With practice, the person can allow the emotional current to pass through their attunement to fundamental consciousness, just as they allowed the imaginary ball to pass through, without flinching or closing against it. Many people will let the emotional current that I produce change their own emotional state—they will feel the emotion as if it were their own. If this happens, they have lost attunement to the field of fundamental consciousness that pervades themselves and me. They have lost contact with themselves and become me. To feel my emotion as if it were their own is very different from having an emotional response to my emotion.

Many sensitive people report that they cannot tell, in their daily lives, if their emotional state is their own or if they have "taken on" the emotional state of people around them. They can become so disoriented by the many emotional states in the environment that they may begin to avoid social interaction. Or they may become martyrs to their sensitivity, making their own hearts and bodies a kind of communal arena. Techniques (such as visualizing a surrounding light) have been developed for sensitive people to protect themselves from the vibrations around them, but these techniques both limit our openness to experience and promote the illusion that the feelings of others can harm us in some way. The vibrations of others can only harm us if we ourselves close our organism against them. When we become stable in our realization of fundamental consciousness, we may feel another person's pain, and respond to it, but we will not feel another person's pain as our own.

In the same way that we need not fear the emotions of others, we can allow our own pain its full depth and movement in the unchanging stillness of fundamental consciousness.

Our true nature can never be injured. We can therefore allow ourselves to be fully available for experience, and our essential being will endure and become even more accessible to us.

CONCLUSION

In this chapter I have described the spatial nature of personal growth. Individuation is a process of increasing our inward contact with ourselves, toward the subtle, vertical core of the body. This deepens our perspective so that we relate to the world across increasing distance. As we achieve this separation from the environment, we also achieve oneness with the environment, because it is through the vertical core of our body that we attune to the pervasive, unified dimension of fundamental consciousness. We access the source, and thus the greatest potency, of our awareness, love, and sensation, in the vertical core of our body. This means that our oneness with the environment is rich with these essential qualities of our being.

We have also seen in this chapter that fundamental consciousness is a dimension of disentanglement from both our internal and external experience of life. It is important to understand that we do not become unfeeling or unthinking zombies, nor does the outer world disappear with this disentanglement. The more disentangled we become, the more fully we pervade our experience, and this makes life richer, deeper, and more vivid.

5
The Body of Clear Space

The realization of fundamental consciousness has a profound effect on the body. It produces a radical shift both in our experience of embodiment, and in the appearance and functioning of our body.

As we become enlightened, we pervade our body as fundamental consciousness. Another way of saying this is that we awaken to the dimension of fundamental consciousness throughout the internal space of our body. This involves letting go of our grip on our body from the essence of our being. It feels as if our essential self is letting go of our false self.

The realization of fundamental consciousness is a gradual process. As we progress in our enlightenment, we gain increasing access to the internal depths of the body, and to the subtle channel that runs through the vertical core of the body. Even with our initial realization, though, we experience a shift from a fragmented sense of our body to a sense of internal wholeness. In the fragmented sense of the body, we can be conscious of our chest but not our legs, for example, or of our head but not our feet, in the same moment. As fundamental consciousness, we experience our whole body (all that we are capable of accessing) at once. In other words, there may be parts of our pelvis, for example, that are too defended to be pervaded by fundamental consciousness, but we will still be able to include the rest of the pelvis in our total body experience. As fundamental consciousness, we also register all of our sensations, emotions, perceptions and cognitions at once, in each moment. We experience each moment with our whole being.

Also, in this subtle dimension of ourselves, we experience our body from the inside. Rather than being conscious of a part of our body, it feels as if the internal space of our body is conscious of itself. We experience no difference, no gap, between our consciousness (our essential self) and our body. It feels like our body is made of consciousness. Our body feels transparent, like empty space, and at the same time it feels full, buoyant, and alive. We have a sense of becoming more present, within our body. Many times I have seen people search for the right word to describe this new experience and finally come up with the word "human." When we pervade our body as fundamental consciousness, we feel more human. We have an actual experience of our existence. This basic sense of existing displaces our anxiety about ourselves, our self-consciousness. Rather than feeling like an object for other people that may be judged or rejected, embodied spiritual awakening is an experience of our body as pure subjectivity.

In this dimension, the body has the receptive and expressive capabilities of consciousness. We are able to receive each moment throughout the internal depth of our body. We experience that each moment occurs inside and outside of our body at the same time, without any gap between inner and outer experience. At the same time, the realized body expresses the many types and shades of human experience, not just in the voice or eyes, but throughout the internal depth of all its parts. For example, a great spiritual master once showed me the embodiment of patience. Without even changing his posture, he suddenly began to emanate, as if through every cell in his body, the quality of patience.

To a sensitive observer, the body of fundamental consciousness looks smooth and unbroken, like a pebble that has been repeatedly washed by the sea. There is an appearance of luminosity and transparency. The internal wholeness of the body makes it more harmonious, and its movements fluid and light. In advanced spiritual masters, these qualities are extreme and easily seen. But even in people who have only begun to realize fundamental consciousness, these changes are visible.

When a person awakens to fundamental consciousness, their eyes and their whole body look more permeable. We can gaze into the depths of a realized body and see the movement of feelings and sensations in that body. A more defended body looks flatter. Both the eyes and the rest of the body have an opaque quality—we cannot look into them as easily.

It is exactly the same with touch. If we touch a more defended body, there is not much sense of depth beneath our hand. But if we touch the body of person who is more open, we can easily feel the whole internal space of that person at once, without changing the position of our hand.

The way we experience our self is also flatter in a more defended body. We cannot feel or sense deeply, and this may make life seem unreal, or meaningless. As we begin to become aware of our self in our defended body, we often feel confined and uncomfortable. Since our breath is contracted along with the rest of our body, we may feel that we are almost suffocating. As we release our defenses, we begin to feel at ease and "at home" in our body.

MISCONCEPTIONS ABOUT THE BODY AND ENLIGHTENMENT

Many spiritual traditions ignore the body, or if they mention it, they say things that may be easily misinterpreted, like "the body drops away." What drops away in enlightenment is the experience of dichotomy between the body and consciousness. The objectified body drops away. And we let go of our grip on our body. In letting go of this grip, however, we drop into the body, all the way through. We become one with the internal space of the body. The contemporary Zen Buddhist philosopher Yuasa (1987) describes embodied consciousness like this, "The 'mind' here is not the surface consciousness, but is the 'mind' that penetrates into the body and deeply subjectivizes it" (p. 105).

When spiritual traditions do not mention the body, practitioners often wind up meditating on the space outside, or above, the body. This prevents them from accessing the vertical core of the body, or allows them to access only the top of the vertical core, severely limiting their realization of fundamental consciousness. The body is our instrument of realization. Enlightenment occurs in and through the body.

Another teaching that may cause confusion about the body is the Hindu Vedantic technique for arriving at fundamental consciousness. Students of Vedanta are taught to say, "I am not my body, I am not my energy, I am not my thoughts." In this way, they recognize that they are nothing that they can point to; rather they are that which does the pointing—the ground itself, pure consciousness. Becoming enlightened shifts our sense of identity from the muscular surface of our body to the most subtle dimension of consciousness pervading our body.

Once I worked with a man who had been a student of Vedanta for many years. He had a teacher in India who had told him that all he had to do was to understand that his true identity was the nondual, all-pervasive Self, and he would be completely enlightened. This intelligent, thoughtful man had spent the past twenty years reading Vedantic literature and trying very hard to understand his true identity. But he felt no more enlightened than when he had first begun.

Working with him, it was obvious that he had a great deal of difficulty breathing. His chest was tight with held grief and his whole body moved up and down as he breathed. It was very difficult for him to contact the internal space of his body. Although he knew exactly what Vedanta said about the true Self, he was far from the subtle experience of nonduality. Spiritual awakening is not just a matter of understanding—it involves self-attunement and the release of defensive rigidities in the body that block self-attunement.

Another misconception is the popular notion, promoted by some Western psychotherapies, that we need to get "out of our head and into our body." This much-used phrase implies that the function of the head is only to produce abstractions and concepts that keep us from experiencing life directly. The word "head" is used to describe static mental ideation. This teaching leads people to hold still or "fog out" their mental faculties, or to work on inhabiting their whole body except for their head. The elimination of the head from our experience of self augments our fragmentation.

It is crucial to our personal growth that we inhabit our head along with the rest of our body. The body of the essential self is a body without static attitudes and beliefs. But the essential self does have a head. As fundamental consciousness, we are still able to recognize, contemplate, and understand our experience. Just as we are able to sense and feel more deeply in the dimension of fundamental consciousness, we are also able to think more clearly. But rather than hanging on to our old or borrowed ideas of life and encountering the world abstractly, we are able to receive new insights and to mature in our understanding.

TRANSFORMATION OF THE BODY: THE SENSES

The body is the instrument of our perception. As our body becomes more subtle, our perception becomes more subtle, too. As we experience our own being as transparent and permeable, everything in our environment also appears to be transparent and permeable.

Enlightenment is thus a refinement of all our senses. It is a seeing through, and a hearing, smelling, tasting, and touching through life--that is, through the dimension of physical matter to the energy and consciousness within. We are able to see the energy in our environment as movement, radiance, and color, to hear it as a subtle buzzing sound and to touch it as vibration and liveliness. We perceive fundamental consciousness in the environment as empty luminous space, pervading everything.

When we realize fundamental consciousness, we experience that instead of five separate senses, we now have one unified medium of perception. As fundamental consciousness, we pervade and reflect all sensory stimuli at once. All of the sights, sounds, tastes, smells, and textures of each moment seem to arise directly out of the empty space, without any effort on our part to perceive them. In the Eastern spiritual literature, this has been called "direct perception" or "bare perception."

Most people have some binding in their sense organs. As children, we constrict our perception to minimize our experience of painful or confusing stimuli. For example, we may constrict our eyes so that we do not see the angry look on our parent's face. Or we may bind the anatomy of our hearing so that we do not hear the sorrowful tone in our parent's voice. Also, some children are discouraged from using their senses fully by adults who feel anxious or ashamed when perceived too clearly. Or by adults who are themselves in denial of an aspect of reality, such as a drinking problem, or a problem in their marriage. The child is then told, directly or indirectly, that her perception is inaccurate. She may even be made to understand that her perception is potentially damaging to the well-being of the family. The child then limits her perception to accommodate the adult's version of reality. We also create ways of focusing our senses that become habitual and which, over time, become rigid limitations in our sense organs.

Because of the underlying unity of the body, a rigidity anywhere within it limits its functioning as a whole. So, in addition to the direct binding of our senses, the defensive structure of our whole body will limit the functioning of our senses. As our body becomes more open, our senses become clearer. We begin to perceive a more vivid world. We also become more sensitive to balance, or harmony.

As we realize fundamental consciousness, our perception functions in a more global way; it reflects all the sensory stimuli of each moment at once. This means that we become more attuned to the relationship between sensory stimuli. For example, we hear the sounds of the birds singing at the same time, and within the same spatial field of consciousness, as we hear the sound of our neighbors laughing, and the sound of the distant lawn mower, and the sound of nearby footsteps on a gravel road. We enter the artist's realm of intervals and counterpoints. Like the artist, we perceive the unity and underlying wholeness of each moment's various shapes, tones, timbres, and textures.

Our senses are also affected by our particular design of openness and defense. For example, if we live mostly in the top of our body, we will see mostly with the top portion of our eyes. People who are intellectually but not emotionally or sensually developed will have this type of visual fragmentation. This limits the visual impression that is received. If we see with only the top portion of our eyes, we will not be sensitive to the emotional depth or sensual texture of the objects or people we see. If we live mostly in the bottom of our body, we will see with mostly the bottom portion of our eyes, and receive mostly sensual or textural information. The reader can test this by looking at an object such as a rug or curtains, and trying to see the texture of the object. If you observe yourself carefully as you do this, you may find that you automatically lower your placement within your body in order to see the texture of the object. If we live mostly in the emotional aspect of our being, we will see mostly with a narrow band in the middle of our eyes. We can only see the whole picture if we see with our whole eyes, and this requires living in our whole body. The same is true for all of our senses.

Exercise 10—Seeing with the Whole Eye

Look at an object in front of you.

Try to see it with only the top portion of your eyes.

Try to see it with only the middle portion of your eyes.

Try to see it with only the bottom portion of your eyes.

Notice how your visual placement changes how you perceive the object. Also notice how the shifts in your visual placement change where you experience yourself in your body.

Now feel that you are inside your whole body all at once. Perceive the object with your whole eyes. Experience that you are seeing the object with your whole body and mind.

You can also observe the visual placement of the people around you. The part of their eyes that they are looking through will tell you where they most experience themselves in their body. Often when two people have difficulty making contact with each other, it is because they are looking at each other from different portions of their eyes—they literally do not see eye to eye.

Exercise 11—Touching with the Whole Body

Feel that you inhabit your whole body at once.

Put your hand on an object, or person.

Feel that you are inside your whole hand, that you inhabit the internal space of your hand.

Touch the object or person staying inside your whole hand.

Two people can practice this exercise by touching each other's hands while inhabiting their own hands. This will increase the contact, and the energy exchange, between the two hands.

Both of these versions of the exercise can be practiced with any part of the body.

ENERGY

Energy is the dynamic aspect of our being, moving through the vast stillness of fundamental consciousness. Our energy system is a complex circulatory system of varying vibrations from gross to subtle. As we realize fundamental consciousness, our energy is able to move more freely through our organism. We are also able to experience a more subtle range of our energy system.

The different subtleties of energy are associated with diverse functions. For example, there is energy associated with organ and other physiological functioning, as described in Chinese and Japanese medicine. There is energy associated with the discharging of emotions, as discussed by Wilhelm Reich and his successors, such as Alexander Lowen and John Pierrakos. As we access the vertical core of the body, we experience our most subtle energy called kundalini in Hindu yoga. We can also experience subtle energy, as a very small vibration within the whole field of fundamental consciousness, inside and outside of our body. Our energy is constantly changing in response to stimuli, to our moods, health, and activity. All of this move-ment occurs in the stillness of fundamental consciousness, without ever changing or disturbing the stillness.

BREATH

As we realize fundamental consciousness, we experience a pro-found change in the way we breathe. We are breathing not just with our respiratory system, but also with the subtle core of our body. This core breath is more refined, smoother and quieter than our ordinary breath, with a subtle electrical or "mental" quality, as if the mind were breathing throughout our whole being. This subtle breath reaches everywhere in our body at once.

Another change that occurs as we begin to inhabit our body fully is that we bring the breath in and out through the center of our nostrils. If we live primarily in the upper third of our body, we will bring the breath in close to the tip of our nose. If we live primarily in the bottom third of our body, we will bring the breath in close to our face. If you take a moment to observe your own breathing, you will see that the part of the nostril you breathe through is related to where you are in your body. You may also find that breathing in and out through the center of your nostrils makes breathing easier.

Exercise 12—Refining the Breath

Here is an exercise to help your breathing become easier and more subtle.

Mentally find the center of your head. The center of the head is between your ears, between your face and the back of your head.

Bring the breath in through the center of the opening of each nostril. Bring the breath all the way into the center of your head on your inhale, and then exhale through the centers of your nostrils. Let the breath be fine and silent—half breath, half mind—so that it can penetrate through your head into the center.

Now bring the breath in through the centers of your nostrils, into the center of your head and down the length of your throat toward your upper chest. On the exhale, bring the breath back up into the center of your head and out your nostrils. Try to actually feel (not visualize) the breath as it moves through you.

Next, bring the breath in through the centers of your nostrils, into the center of your head, down your throat and into your lungs, filling the lungs with breath. On your exhale, bring the breath back up into the center of your head and out your nostrils.

Bring the breath in through the centers of your nostrils, into the center of your head, down your throat, into your lungs, and then into your whole body. Feel that the breath reaches and nourishes every cell in every part of your body. On your exhale, bring the breath back to the center of your head and out your nostrils.

Most important in this exercise is that the breath passes through the center of your head on both your inhale and your exhale. When the breath passes through the center of the head (or through any part of our subtle core) it becomes refined and integrated with our subtle energy. In that refined condition, it can reach everywhere in the body. As you practice, let the breath be smooth and effortless.

It is important not to attempt to breathe this way, or to manipulate your breath in any way, all the time. Practice the exercise and then let go of it. It is meant to refine your breath so that your spontaneous breathing pattern gradually becomes more subtle and pervasive.

The breath is one of the most obvious bridges between inner and outer experience. The binding in the body diminishes our ability to breathe freely and easily. Neither our consciousness nor our breath have access to the rigid, defended parts of our body. Also, just as with our senses, most of us have directly defended our breath so as not to feel our own pain or take in the painful emotions around us.

Our breathing pattern was formed in relation to our childhood environment. But we cannot be present in ourselves unless we breathe the air that is here now. This process of coming into the present with our breath is an important component of spiritual awakening. It is part of opening to and directly experiencing our oneness with the environment.

SPEECH

Many people have told me that it is most difficult for them to remain in the dimension of fundamental consciousness when they are speaking. The anxiety that many people have about verbal expression creates an automatic defensive contraction in the throat in preparation for speech that blocks attunement to fundamental consciousness. We can maintain attunement to fundamental consciousness while speaking by consciously inhabiting our neck, vocal mechanism, and the subtle core of the neck. The voice becomes more authentically expressive when we inhabit our vocal anatomy, making it easier to convey our true thoughts and feelings. We also feel safer when we inhabit our body because we have a felt sense of our own existence. It is less likely that we will feel the need to defend our voice if we experience the quality of our being while we are speaking, or about to speak.

The two most common defenses in preparation for speech are contracting downward in the neck, toward the chest, and contracting upward from the neck into the head. It is helpful in both cases to consciously inhabit the upper chest, as well as the neck. If we experience that we are "sitting in our heart" while we speak, it will keep us from leaping up into our head or pressing down against our chest and obstructing our breath.

GRAVITY AND BALANCE

Another important shift that occurs in our body as we realize fundamental consciousness is in our relationship with gravity. In this chapter I will describe how the shift in our relationship with gravity affects the body. In the next chapter, I will discuss this shift in terms of our relationship with the cosmos.

Before we realize fundamental consciousness, we experience our body as a solid mass of physical matter, rigidly separate from the environment. We therefore experience gravity as a force outside of our body that pulls us to the ground as we struggle to remain upright. This struggle against gravity results in chronically held muscles, which limit our movement and cause pain and exhaustion.

As we begin to experience our self and our body as the empty space of fundamental consciousness rather than as material solidity, we become open to the force of gravity throughout the internal depth of ourselves. This is another way of saying that we are able to relax within the internal space of our body. As we become more relaxed, we also become increasingly balanced throughout our whole being. Balance is alignment with Earth's gravity. As we let go of our defensive grip on ourselves, we naturally settle into a balanced state within our whole being.

The balance that occurs as we open to gravity involves the entire internal content and spectrum of our being. We are more balanced physically, our energy circulates more evenly, the functions of the two hemispheres of our brain are more balanced and integrated, as we become open to the self-existent expanse of fundamental consciousness. Fundamental consciousness is the dimension of absolute balance. It is motionless because it is balanced.

As we surrender to gravity throughout our whole being, our energy currents move through us more deeply and freely. Among other currents, we can experience both a downward current through our body that feels like it comes from above us, and an upward current that comes up from the ground. This upward current makes the body light and buoyant. It supports us, when we are sitting or standing. There is actually no need for us to hold ourselves upright. The more we settle (internally) to the ground, the more we experience this upward force. The more we let go of ourselves, the more this upward current supports us.

Exercise 13—Opening to the Upward Current

Here is an exercise to help you experience the upward current in your body. This current is extremely subtle and may take some practice to experience.

Stand, barefoot, on a level floor.

Feel that you are inside your whole body all at once, including your feet.

Feel that there is no separation between you and the floor.

Mentally find the centers of the soles of your heels.

Balance your awareness of these two points—find them both at exactly the same time.

Open these centers to the current that rises upward from the ground. This current rises through everywhere in your feet, but it enters most easily through the centers of the soles of your heels. Do not force or pull the current upward, but subtly attune to its spontaneous upward movement.

Find the inside of your hip sockets. Balance your awareness of your hip sockets; find them both at the same time. Feel that the hip sockets rest toward the centers of the soles of your heels. Receive the upward current inside your hip sockets.

Find the center of your head (the center of the internal space of your head, between your ears). Feel that the center of your head is resting toward the ground. Receive the upward current inside your head. The current rises up from below the centers of the soles of your heels and from below the center of the bottom of your torso.

Allow the current to keep moving out through the center of the top of your head.

Keep letting go of your grip on yourself and settling toward the ground, as you open to this upward movement.

The body of fundamental consciousness is light and buoyant, but it is also internally relaxed and settled to the ground. Some people experience themselves as shorter, or heavier, as they realize fundamental consciousness because they feel closer to the ground. For people whose placement of consciousness has been mostly in their upper body and head, this connectedness with the ground can be uncomfortable at first. But the "airborne" quality that they had in their fragmented placement will now rise up from below their feet and the bottom of their torso, rather than lifting the top of their body away from the bottom.

Exercise 14—Balance

Here is an exercise to help you attune to the balance of fundamental consciousness.

Mentally locate the space to the right of you.

Mentally locate the space to the left of you.

Now mentally locate the space to the right and the left of you at the same time.

Mentally locate the space in front of you.

Mentally locate the space behind you.

Now mentally locate the space in front and behind you at the same time.

You may notice that when you balance your attunement to the space around you, you automatically arrive in the vertical core of your body. To be balanced is also to be centered.

HEALTH AND HEALING

Although the body is always transformed by our realization of fundamental consciousness, we do not need a perfect physical body in order to become enlightened. A body that is disabled or ill can also be an instrument of spiritual awakening. Even very advanced masters are seen to succumb to sickness, old age, and death. However, anyone can access the subtle core of their being and the dimension of fundamental consciousness, regardless of their physical condition.

Although the realization of fundamental consciousness does not necessarily eliminate disablement or severe illness, it does offer some effective, subtle ways of healing the body. Subtle healing methods almost always take longer than conventional medicine, but they can sometimes heal what other approaches cannot. Subtle healing methods also effect a transformation of all levels of our being, so that our illness or injury becomes a path toward deeper enlightenment.

Chinese medicine views all illness and injury as a reflection of blockages in our energy system. If we attune to fundamental consciousness in the area that is blocked, energy will begin to flow there again. One way to do this is as follows.

Exercise 15—Subtle Healing

A – Mentally locate the center of your head.

From the center of your head, mentally find the area of your body that is ill or injured. If there is a particular area of pain, tension, or numbness, focus into the center of this area. You are finding the area from the center of your head so that you can attune to the dimension of fundamental consciousness in that area. This is not a visualization exercise. Try to actually experience yourself in the center of your head and the area of illness.

Hold your attention steady in the center of your head and in the area of illness or injury, and breathe smoothly and evenly through your nose. You may feel subtle movement within the area of tension or illness as it releases.

B – Another subtle healing method is through balance. For example, if you feel pain in one side of your jaw, you can attune to the area of pain and the other side of your jaw at the same time. This will help you let go of the tension in your jaw.

Both these exercises can help you contact the dimension of your being that is beyond illness or injury. Fundamental consciousness is our uncontracted self. In this dimension there is no tension, and therefore no pain. By contacting fundamental consciousness in a particular part of the body, we can more easily let go of the physical rigidity and energy blockages in that area.

Except in the case of mild, recent injury or tension, this type of healing usually requires repeated, consistent practice over time to be effective. In the case of illness or severe injury, it should be combined with more immediate healing methods. We often become ill or injured in exactly the area of our being that we most need to awaken for our wholeness. To begin to gain consciousness and energy flow in an ill or injured area is thus important for our personal growth, even if we are not able to entirely alleviate our physical condition.

PHYSICAL SENSATION

In our culture, most of us live more in the upper part of our body than in our pelvis and legs. In this fragmented condition, we can experience awareness and emotion, but not very much physical sensation. For this reason, when some people speak of being "in the body," they are really referring to gaining the capacity for physical sensation.

Physical sensation is not just a capacity; it is a quality, a part of our essential (unconstructed) experience of being. As I explained in chapter 2, fundamental consciousness is made of the essential qualities of our whole being. In Realization Process, physical sensation is considered an essential quality of both our internal wholeness and our oneness with our environment. It is an intrinsic aspect of our communion with everything around us. It is also part of our unified sense perception, a "transpersonal" or pervasive sense of touch. As fundamental consciousness, for example, we can feel and resonate with the physical sensations of other people without actually touching them.

It is often our physical sensation and sexuality that are wounded and repressed in childhood. Any situation that prohibits or unduly limits our vitality, budding sexuality, or power will affect our level of physical sensation by causing us to constrict the bottom third of our body. Typically, cultural taboos against sexual feelings are transmitted to children by sexually repressed adults. Also, sexual abuse of children by adults, either overt or more subtly intrusive, leaves children with deep-rooted trauma and defense in their capacity for sensation.

Diminished physical sensation is also a legacy of traditional religions, particularly in the West, that emphasize the transcendent "otherworldly" aspect of religious experience and focus on the cultivation of love and awareness. This religious focus has resulted in a general alienation in our culture from the body and from nature. The realization of fundamental consciousness is both immanent and transcendent at the same time, and contains as an inseparable unity the qualities of awareness, love, and physical sensation.

MOVEMENT

The transformation of the body in fundamental consciousness naturally transforms the way we move. Instead of moving with only our superficial muscle structure, we experience that we are moving through the whole internal depth of our body. This means that we move with all the dimensions of our being—physical matter, energy, and fundamental consciousness, and with all the essential qualities of fundamental consciousness—awareness, emotion, and physical sensation. It is important that we practice moving through the dimension of fundamental consciousness so that we can move through the activities of our life without losing our realization. This is not just a practice of being mindful of our movements, but of moving with our fundamental being.

Exercise 16—Moving as Fundamental Consciousness

A – One of the ways that the dimension of fundamental consciousness can be accessed in the body is through the joints. This exercise uses the centers of the wrists.

Sit in a chair or cross-legged on a pillow. Rest your hands on your legs, with the palms down.

Mentally find the center of your head, between your ears, and between your face and the back of your head.

From the center of your head, find the inside of both wrists (the center of the internal space of each wrist).

Balance your awareness of the inside of both wrists—find the inside of both wrists at the same time.

Staying in the center of your head, and the inside of both wrists, slowly lift your hands, palms down, toward your chest. Match the quality inside your wrists to the quality inside the center of your head as you move.

Staying inside the center of your head and inside both wrists, slowly turn your hands palm up and bring them back down toward your legs.

B – Here is an exercise for accessing and moving through— or as—fundamental consciousness within your whole body.

Stand, preferably barefoot. Feel that you are inside your feet, that you inhabit your feet. Feel that you are inside your ankles. Experience the internal continuity between your ankles and your feet.

Feel that you inhabit your legs, your torso, your shoulders, arms and hands, your neck and head. This does not mean to be aware of the space inside the body, but to actually be that space. Experience that you are the internal space of each part of your body.

Feel that you inhabit your whole body at once. Attune to the quality of your self inside your whole body. Let yourself feel that there is no difference between your body and your self. Your self is standing there.

Move your arms, staying attuned to the quality of self. The internal space of your arms is moving through the space of the room.

Now move your whole body through space, staying inside your whole body and attuned to the quality of self.

You can also practice staying inside your whole body, and attuned to the quality of your self, as you walk slowly across the room. Observe yourself to see which parts of your body you lose contact with as you walk, and practice inhabiting those parts of yourself.

Conclusion

When we are attuned to fundamental consciousness throughout our whole body, we embody the essence of our being. We experience that we exist as an individual form, that we take up space, and that we are also permeable and continuous with the space that pervades our environment. Our being feels both entirely empty, like an empty vessel, and, at the same time, vibrantly alive. We feel that we are made of consciousness, all the way through the space of our body. We also feel that we are made of the essential qualities inherent in fundamental consciousness: awareness, love, and physical sensation. From the depths of our own being, we can connect with the depths of everyone and everything around us. We begin to experience a whole body, whole being relationship with all of the other forms of life that we encounter.

Inhabiting the internal space of the body is the basis of a true sense of self-possession, and self-confidence. It always produces a shift in the way we feel about ourselves. It is impossible for us to hate ourselves, for example, if we experience that we are made of love. We also feel less overwhelmed by our environment when we have an actual experience of our existence within our body. Inward contact with ourselves also affects how we treat our body, with regard to food, sexual relationships, rest, air and other environmental conditions. As we are able to inhabit more of the internal space of our body, our realization of fundamental consciousness continues to deepen. It feels as if we are disappearing into empty space, and, at the same time, it feels as if our individual form is gradually being born.

6
Person and Cosmos

*The whole universe is of one and the
same root as my own self, and all things
are one with me.*

—Seng Chao

We have seen how fundamental consciousness is the basis of both our individual wholeness, and the unity of our internal and external experience. It is also the basis of an even more mysterious experience: a sense of oneness with the universe. This oneness is beyond the awe we may feel for the beauty and grandeur of the cosmos. It is a felt sense that the essence of our being extends beyond the sky and the surface of the earth, that it is somehow larger and more subtle than the material world. It is a felt sense that our own essence is the same unbounded essence of the universe. This is not an energetic expansion of our individual being, but the experience of our own presence as inseparable from the vast presence pervading everywhere.

Many spiritual teachings refer to the oneness of the individual and the universe. The Tibetan Buddhist teacher Namkhai

Norbu (1986) writes, "When one realizes oneself, one realizes the essential nature of the universe. The existence of duality is only an illusion and when the illusion is undone, the primordial unity of one's own nature and the nature of the universe is realized, or made real" (p. 124).

One of the main texts of the Kashmir Shaivism school of Hinduism says, "The yogi has an experience in which he is inwardly absorbed in the Supreme Divine consciousness (nimilana); again when he turns toward the universe, he experiences it as the same as his own essential Divine consciousness (unmilana)" (Singh, 1979, pp. 231–32).

And Shankara, the great sage of the Advaita Vedanta school of Hinduism wrote, "The Supreme Brahman (pure consciousness) pervades the entire universe…and shines of Itself" (Nikhilananda, 1989, p. 167) (parentheses added).

My perspective, as I've emphasized throughout the book, is that we are in a process of completing our contact with our individual being at the same time that we are in a process of becoming (or realizing that we are) entirely one with the essential nature of the universe. In practical terms, this means that as we realize oneness, the experience of I and other is actually becoming clearer, more authentic. Our sense of relationship and dialogue with other people becomes less veiled by projection and defense, allowing for greater connection and intimacy. When two people meet each other in the dimension of fundamental consciousness, they experience both oneness—the sense that they are made of the unified space that pervades them both—and a deeper, more fluid exchange with each other.

The same coemergence of relationship and oneness seems to occur in our relationship with the spiritual essence of the universe.

To speak about having a relationship with the "universe" is necessarily to engage in speculation. I want to make clear that I am not trying to propose a metaphysical system. It cannot be known with certainty if fundamental consciousness really does pervade the whole universe or, if it does, what effect that has on our individual lives. The ideas in this chapter come from my experience of a relationship with a spiritual otherness that I have had since childhood and that grows more accessible as I progress on my spiritual path. Many others have also experienced this relationship, in the form of responses to their prayers, desires, and intentions, and in a sense of connection with a vast presence. Although these events can easily be ridiculed by people who have not experienced them, I believe that they are too central to spiritual awakening to ignore. This chapter is about the significance that these experiences may have for the process of enlightenment.

I do not mean that this spiritual presence necessarily has knowledge or will of its own, that it is a deity outside of nature, although of course that is possible. In my own life, I have come to conceive of it as consciousness that pervades all forms in nature, but that only reaches the ability to know itself in human beings.

Many people have experienced cosmic responsiveness in moments of peak illumination or intense need. When we begin to realize fundamental consciousness, however, this responsiveness can become an ongoing aspect of our lives. As fundamental consciousness, we are beginning to experience that the wisdom and creativity of the universe are our own wisdom and creativity. This means that to call on a vast cosmic intelligence is to call on our own essential being: the one being of the universe. To ask the universe for something is, in a sense, to create it ourselves.

We can also feel a deeper love for, and from, the universe. This is an experience of relationship, of duality. But at the same time, we recognize that the love that seems to pervade the universe is the same love that pervades our own being. We experience that our own being is made of the fundamental love of the universe.

This chapter also explores how fundamental consciousness, pervading the universe, may propel the process of our growth toward complete enlightenment. It has often been observed that both psychological healing and spiritual realization are spontaneous, natural processes.

The process of enlightenment is facilitated by letting go of any manipulation or veiling of reality. When we first achieve spiritual oneness, we feel that we are entering a dimension of existence that has always been there, that we are experiencing our true nature. The discovery of fundamental consciousness as our underlying true nature suggests that we are already unified with the cosmos in this dimension of ourselves, even before we realize it. I will now describe three ways in which our fundamental unity may impel our process toward complete enlightenment. These are: through stimulation, synchronicity, and gravity.

1. STIMULATION

The infant is born with the potential for intelligence, love, and sensual pleasure. But we know that this potential will not develop without a mother's (or primary caretaker's) love and attention. A neglected infant suffers psychological and developmental deficits and may even die from lack of nurture. Thus, from the very beginning of life, we are dependent upon the environment to awaken our most basic capacities. As Daniel

N. Stern (1985) documents, we grow in our self-knowledge and our ability to communicate with others within the matrix of the child-parent relationship.

Children develop their capacities as they learn the world around them. They imitate other people and they are faced with a variety of sensory stimuli and cognitive challenges that elicit new levels of functioning and integration. Another component of stimulation is more subtle, but just as crucial for the child's growth. This component can be called "direct transmission." This term is used to describe the expansion of consciousness that occurs for spiritual students in the presence of their teacher's expanded consciousness. It is a process of vibratory resonance and stimulation. In the same way that a spiritual master expands his or her students just by being with them, the parent's love stimulates and deepens the child's capacity for love. The parent's awareness stimulates the child's awareness. And the parent's physical sensation stimulates the child's sensation.

The child's openness is also transmitted to the parents. But, although children love without inhibition, they do not love with the intensity or depth of an adult. Likewise, their capacity for awareness and physical sensation, although unfettered, are still in a rudimentary state.

Just as children must inevitably receive a somewhat skewed education from their somewhat imperfect parents, they will also be unevenly stimulated by their parents' transmission of their own pattern of openness and defense. For example, a mother who is very loving but constricted in her sensuality will be able to stimulate her child's love, but not her child's capacity for physical sensation. Of course, in addition to this automatic transmission of the parents' limitations, children are also making their own defenses against the painful circumstances in their environment. So, as they are awakening to life, they are also closing off to life. The parts of themselves that they close off will not be as available for subsequent stimulation from the environment.

As children continue to mature, other influences come into their lives and contribute to their growth. In the expanded environment of school and other activities, they continue to learn about themselves and the world, and they continue to be awakened by the awareness, love, and sensation of the life around them.

We can also consider that the essential awareness, love, and sensation inherent in the fundamental consciousness of the universe stimulates and awakens the potentials of our being in the same way as do the other people in our environment. This vast consciousness is transmitted to us through nature. It is like a great spiritual master in whose presence we are always living. As we become more open—as our internal contact with ourselves deepens—we become more sensitive to this transmission. We may experience it first as a communion with a presence outside of ourselves, in nature, or beyond the sky. But all the while, this vast consciousness is stimulating our contact with ourselves toward the core of our being, where we finally recognize our oneness with it.

Exercise 17—Cultivating a Relationship with the Cosmos

Sit or stand upright. Find the center of your head (between your ears, in the center of the internal space of your head.) When you find the center of your head, you will feel an automatic resonance down through the whole subtle core of your body.

From the center of your head (staying in the center of your head), mentally find a point as far in the distance in front of you as you can. This is not a projection of focus; you are finding the point from, and with, the center of your head.

You can direct prayers, or questions to this point in the distance.

You can do this same exercise from the point in the subtle core of your chest (your heart chakra).

Exercise 18—Attuning to Oneness with the Cosmos

Stand or sit outside in a country setting, with your eyes open. Begin with the end of Exercise 1: feel that you are inside your whole body. Find the space outside your body. Experience that the space inside and outside your body is the same, continuous space.

Bring your focus upward to the sky. Experience that the space that pervades you also pervades the sky.

Bring your focus down to the ground. Experience that the space that pervades you also pervades the earth. If you are at the seaside, feel that the space that pervades you also pervades the ocean.

Feel that the space that pervades you also pervades the whole environment.

2. Synchronicity

Another way in which the universe seems to propel our growth process is through synchronicity, the correspondence between our external circumstances and our internal life, such as our mental and emotional states, needs, and desires. This means that we often find ourselves with exactly the right circumstances to help release and resolve our bound pain, and exactly the right teachers or practices that we need for our spiritual development.

Recently, the understanding that we can influence our circumstances with our desires or intentions has produced both extremely simplistic interpretations and vitriolic denials in our popular media. There is a striking polarity in our "new age" culture between those who think that they just have to intend to have a Mercedes and one will arrive at their doorstep, and those who think that all desire and self-gratification are the antithesis of spiritual life. I see this as a new guise for an old debate between the hedonist and Puritan perspectives that have helped shape America from its beginning. In my view, the universe does respond to our conscious intentions sometimes, but there are many other factors involved in producing our circumstances. Synchronicity is a subtle phenomenon, usually occurring unbidden, and often in response to needs and mental states that are unconscious or barely conscious.

The correspondences between inner and outer experience can imbue life with an eerily dreamlike, symbolic quality. For example, I remember an incident when I gave a talk to a group of people who were particularly skeptical about spiritual experience. I managed to stay fairly calm throughout the barrage of criticism that followed my talk, listening carefully to their objections. But immediately afterward, I got locked in the bathroom down the hall from the meeting room; a doorknob on the outside of the door had fallen off. I banged loudly on the door and yelled for assistance for some time before anyone heard me. For the first time that afternoon, I felt my distress at their having "turned a deaf ear" to my presentation.

People who observe their lives carefully realize that these synchronistic events occur too frequently to be viewed as simple coincidences. Even the scientific community is beginning to study this strange phenomenon. A recent article in the *Journal of Consciousness Studies,* for example, attempts to find the possible "quantum mechanical" basis for it. The authors describe events of synchronicity as "transporting a message of vital relevance for the persons involved and that they usually occur in situations of high emotional tension and receptivity for the meaning of such messages" (Lucador, Romer & Walach, 2007, p. 51).

Synchronicity often functions to bring us the necessary circumstances for our healing or growth. For example, we may be working on feeling less intimidated by other people, and a situation arises at work in which it is necessary for us to confront our boss. Synchronicity also occurs with frequency in events that are not highly important or emotionally charged. For example, we may need to ask a friend a question, and run into her on our way to work. We may be trying to think of the name of a particular artist, and soon after, see the name in a magazine article.

Another example is the synchronicity that played a part in my obtaining the article that I just quoted. One evening, my husband was reading through this manuscript. Although we have been on the spiritual path together for many years, Zoran is also a scientist; he researches the neural correlates of consciousness. And he comes from an atheistic family background, as I do. He told me that he was concerned that I would appear naïve if I included this section on synchronicity. Later that evening, however, he happened to be visiting the website of a journal that is quite respected in his field. While looking for information that he needed for his own writing, he came across the article titled "Synchronistic Phenomena as Entanglement Correlations in Generalized Quantum Theory." Interestingly, the authors of this scientific paper are not even trying to determine if synchronicity exists. They are attempting to understand how it functions.

There is a dichotomy in metaphysical thought that mirrors the debate being played out in our media today. One school counsels us to receive humbly and gratefully all that comes our way. It teaches that we should surrender our own small will to the will of God, having faith that there is wisdom and purpose even in our misfortunes. The other school says that we ourselves are the creators of our circumstances. Even our most painful situations occur because we ourselves desire and will them. This school also maintains that by focusing intently on a visualization of our desired future, we can, to the extent that we have mastered this ability, consciously create the life circumstances of our own choice.

Although these two philosophies seem, on the surface, incompatible, I believe that there is truth in both of them. Many of the desires that create our circumstances are the old unfulfilled desires of our childhood that are buried beyond our conscious reach within our body. Our conscious acceptance of the unfolding of this buried content may help us learn and grow from circumstances that would otherwise seem intolerable to us.

The contents of our bound childhood pain emerge into the arena of daily life in order for the bound emotions to be expressed, and for the unmet needs to be fulfilled or resolved. For example, I worked with a woman whose greatest childhood wounds were the sudden death of her father when she was seven, followed by the death of her mother when she was sixteen. She came to me because her husband's fatal heart attack several years before had left her so shattered that she was still unable to function at work or as a mother. His death had left her with the same bleak despair and sense of utter helplessness that she had felt as a child at the death of her parents. In order to overcome the crisis of losing her husband, she had to complete the mourning process for her parents that she had been too alone and afraid to experience as a child. She had to acknowledge and express her conflicted emotions of grief and anger at these losses, and the guilt she felt at surviving and going on with her life.

Many psychological theorists have remarked on the correspondences between our psychological history and our circumstances. Sigmund Freud was fascinated by our tendency to find ourselves in the same painful circumstance repeatedly. He called this phenomenon "repetition compulsion" and described it as "the manifestation of the power of the repressed" (1961, p. 14). He based psychoanalysis on the client's compulsion to project his painful relationship with his parents onto the therapist, thus repeating, or attempting to repeat, the painful circumstances of his childhood in the therapist's office. Arnold Mindell's (1985) Process Therapy describes a similar notion that the client will "dream up" the therapist, actually influencing him to behave in ways that resemble his parents' behavior toward him in his childhood. Harville Hendrix (1988, p. 9) claims that we choose our mate based on our unresolved child-hood needs. He suggests that what he calls the "old brain" holds our painful childhood memories and watches for a potential mate with the familiar attributes of our parents.

Although most theorists explain the correspondence between childhood pain and adult circumstances as the result of subconscious attraction and choice, it appears from the intimate details we learn of our client's lives over the years that many situations do not fit into this category. It seems that there may be some more subtle mechanism at work. It is interesting to read Freud's struggle to remain "rational" in light of his own observations. He writes, "We are more impressed by the cases where the subject appears to have a passive experience, over which he has no influence, but in which he meets with a repetition of the same fatality" (1961, p. 16). On the following page he offers a somewhat qualified contradiction of this statement: "A great deal of what might be described as the compulsion of destiny seems intelligible on a rational basis; so that we are under no necessity to call in a new and mysterious motive force to explain it." But in his choice of the words "a great deal," he seems to leave a margin of doubt about his own rationale.

Freud did not seem to view the repetition compulsion as a part of a natural healing process, but rather as a symptom of neurosis. But I suggest that it may be an aspect of our healthy, ongoing relationship with our potential wholeness. By whole-ness, I mean the realization of fundamental consciousness throughout our whole body. Many people who observe their growth process carefully report that as they come to a new area of work on themselves, events in their life emerge to bring them the means to facilitate this work. An illustration of this was a woman who, as a child, had been repeatedly told to be quiet and not disturb the adults with her "silly chatter." When I first met her she was very subdued and spoke almost in a whisper. Shortly after I began working with her, she was looking for work as a dance therapist, with little success. Just as she was ready to give up, a job became available at a nursing home for a music therapist. Although she had no experience as a music therapist, the home's director offered her the job. As a music therapist she was required, almost daily, to lead the nursing home residents in song. This activity helped loosen the tension that she had held in her throat for so many years.

I have described how the unfolding of events may respond to the desires and needs of our childhood mentality buried in our body. This process may also respond to our conscious desires, if we focus our will with enough intensity. However, our conscious desires are often in conflict with our unconscious desires, and this diminishes our creative power. For example, I worked with a woman whose greatest desire was to get married. She made a daily practice of visualizing herself meeting the right man and happily settling down with him. Although she approached this practice with determination, she often found it difficult to get a clear image of herself as happily married. She finally realized that she had an old image of married life that entirely contradicted this happy picture. The old image was based on her memory of her mother, married to an alcoholic and raising four children, of her crying and threatening to leave, and then crying even more bitterly because she felt she could never leave. The fear of being trapped in an intolerable situation like her mother prevented this woman from whole-heartedly visualizing herself as married.

The view that our circumstances are the result of our desires has come under fire from people dealing with severe physical illness. They say that this idea makes them feel ashamed of becoming ill, as if their illness showed some lack of willpower. It must be recognized that the causes of illness, and other circumstances as well, are complex, with many contributing factors.

However, to the extent that illness is caused by psychological conditions, it is not only, or even primarily, the present emotional or mental state that is responsible. Emotional pain, when held in the body for many years, can cause severe imbalances and blockages in our energy circulation, and may eventually lead to illness. This is in no way a sign of weakness on the part of the sufferer. No one is entirely without bound childhood pain in their body. But it does mean that there is the possibility of healing through the release of these psychological holding patterns. Besides healing through the release of bound emotional pain, some people have been able to heal themselves through visualization and prayer, and through attunement to fundamental consciousness. This ability is part of our human potential.

Although we can use our creative power to influence our lives, it is also important to surrender to the spontaneous aspect of our growth process. Tibetan Buddhism teaches that the practice of visualization should always end with dissolving the image into empty consciousness. The release of the visualization is as important for its effectiveness as the visualization itself. Creativity cannot occur without receptivity.

It is important to be carefully attuned to our desires, for they help form our individual path toward wholeness. Desire

arises out of tension. We project our desire onto material pos-
sessions, etc., but we can also see through these superficial
attractions to our more essential desire to be free from the tension of our incompleteness. Desire can be understood as the
force of our will toward equilibrium and wholeness.

As the unconscious desires of our bound childhood mentality become resolved, our circumstances begin to match our
conscious desires. We become less fragmented, and our desire
also becomes less fragmented. We begin to experience that we
desire wholeness, that we crave connection with our self and
others, that we want to penetrate through the numb parts of
ourselves to the life within them. At this point, we find ourselves with opportunities to work directly on our spiritual
awakening.

The desire/response aspect of our relationship with the universe is often dismissed as the worst sort of new-age babble. It
can easily be labeled "magical thinking," one of psychology's
worst insults, because it does point to a magical aspect of nature.
But this is magic that goes on all the time in our lives, and may
simply be a basic principle of the nature of the universe. Hindu
metaphysics calls the universe a "wish-fulfilling gem."

3. GRAVITY

Fundamental consciousness is the dimension of perfect balance. As our enlightenment progresses, we become increasingly
balanced throughout the internal space of our whole being.
Balance is our alignment with Earth's gravitational field. Wherever we have closed our organism against life's stimulation, we
are out of balance.

As I said in the last chapter, gravity moves not on us but through us, because we are not solid objects but open vibrational fields. As we release our defensive grip on ourselves, we can settle the weight of our whole internal being to the ground. This helps relax our habitual patterns of overstimulation or excessive charge in our nervous system. Overexcitement of our intellect or heart can cause fixity of focus in those areas that fragment our being. But as we surrender our weight to gravity, these loci of agitation also let go. With this internal letting go, we can experience a current rising upward from below us, through the space of our body. We can feel this upward rising force pushing against our defensive skews, like water pushing against a barrier. As we become more open to this movement, we become more balanced. Openness, balance, and enlightenment are synonymous.

The role of gravity in our process of enlightenment makes relaxation an important part of spiritual practice. It also shows the importance of sleep for our natural growth process. In sleep, our body is at its most relaxed. This may explain why there is often spontaneous emergence and resolution of our bound pain in our dreams. Just as the stimulation of the universe, and the responsiveness of the universe, bring our bound pain to our awareness, surrendering to gravity also helps penetrate our binding and brings its contents to awareness.

SPONTANEITY

Many schools of psychological and spiritual thought recognize the spontaneity of the growth process. Rebirthing and EMDR (Eye Movement Desensitization and Reprocessing therapy), for example, are ways to promote the natural unwinding of the knotted skein of our holding patterns. In general, a new understanding is dawning in psychotherapy that cautions the therapist to follow the lead of the client's process as she or he presents it in the session, rather than approach the client with a fixed diagnosis and treatment plan.

Zen Buddhism teaches a meditation called Shikan-taza, which is the practice of sitting still without any particular object of concentration. It is taught that just sitting still and breathing will gradually unfold the meditator toward enlightenment. The Zen teacher and scholar Philip Kapleau (1980) wrote, "The very foundation of Shikan-taza is an unshakable faith that sitting as the Buddha sat, with the mind void of all conceptions, of all beliefs and points of view, is the actualization of unfoldment of the inherently enlightened Bodhi-mind with which all are endowed" (p. 7).

The Dzog-chen school of Tibetan Buddhism teaches the same technique of just sitting still as the mind gradually clears and realizes itself as fundamental consciousness. The Tibetan Buddhist teacher Chogyam Trungpa Rinpoche (1972) wrote, ". . . one can free oneself like a snake unwinding" (p. 25).

The imagery of unwinding is often used to describe the nature of personal growth. I have observed that the bound pain in our body really is a coil, a twisting away from life. And each area of buried memory and pain contains the tension of that twist. As in archery, when the bow is pulled taut to release the arrow, the held tensions in our body also contain the momentum for their return to their origin, once the process of release has begun. This momentum, released through stimulation, synchronicity, and the movement of gravity, produces the spontaneous unfolding of our path toward wholeness.

Even terrible events, such as wars and famines, may be viewed as both the symptoms and the working through, on a large scale, of the imbalances and rigidities bound in the bodies and minds of human beings, and the greed, hatred, and general limitation in one's scope of awareness that may result from these rigidities.

PROJECTIONS ONTO GOD

Just as we can gradually see through the projections of our childhood family onto our present relationships, we can see through and dissolve the projections that obscure our relationship with the universe. Most of us have been forming since childhood some (usually unconscious) notion of the source of fortune and misfortune, some image of God. God is often presented to children in the guise of a distant parental figure, with the power to punish and reward. It is easy to project onto a parental image of God, the imperfect, conditional love that we received from our parents. For example, I worked with a man who had a deep-rooted sense of not belonging anywhere, and of being rejected by God. He could not imagine good things happening to him, because he knew that God did not want him to be happy. He was resistant to experiencing fundamental consciousness pervading his body, because he did not want to try to feel connected to something that had rejected him. As I got to know him better, I learned that he had been sent away to live at a boarding school when he was three years old for the duration of his childhood, even though both his parents were alive. He had never, even as a child, allowed himself to feel his pain and confusion at this rejection, but instead directed his sense of alienation toward God.

Often, dualistic religious teachings imply that we must beg God for our well-being and good fortune. At worst, we are taught that God does not want us to be whole; that he frowns on sexuality, self-expression, and self-love. I worked with a woman who told me that she had rebelled against God in order to be herself. Unfortunately, she paid a high price for this rebellion. Although she felt independent, she was unable to feel like a good person because she felt in conflict with God. She presented a flamboyant "bad" persona that masked a deeper sense of shame and self-loathing. Even more troubling for her was a sense of being cut off from God, from her true relationship with the universe and her deep spiritual self. But she was convinced that to feel this connection, she would have to give up both her sexuality and her right to think for herself. As she began to examine her life history, however, she realized that it was in her childhood home and her Sunday school classes that her sensual vitality and her developing opinions were rejected.

We also make positive projections onto the universe, for example imagining it as the Mother or the all-forgiving Jesus. These projections can be helpful at points in our development because they may provide useful metaphors for our relationship with the universe. But even these images must eventually be dropped in order for us to realize our oneness with the cosmos. There is a story that the great Hindu spiritual master Ramakrishna used to worship a stone carving of Krishna. One day he dreamed that his teacher appeared to him and rubbed the stone against Ramakrishna's forehead until finally, in great pain, he promised to give up this dualistic spiritual practice.

As we let go of our projections, we begin to experience the mysterious benevolence of the universe. We are able to receive its nurture and rely on its laws of evolution. We can surrender to the natural unfolding of events in our life, and to the pervasive awareness, love, and sensation at the root of our being. As Karlfried Graf Durckheim (1962) writes, "Faith is innate in every man thanks to the bond which unites him with the ground of Being" (p. 11). The faith that so many of us have lost in our conflict with the God of our childhood returns with the realization of fundamental consciousness, not just as belief, but as a quality of our being.

I have found that many psychological problems that do not seem affected by our awareness of their childhood origin will finally heal when we experience our relationship with the universe. One woman came to me because she had been eating compulsively all her life. She was able to uncover the source of her problem; she was well aware that she had substituted food for her mother's ambivalent love, but she continued to eat far beyond her physical hunger. She was terrified that the feeling of not being loved would destroy her if she did not keep filling her emotional emptiness with food. It was not until she realized fundamental consciousness, and could actually feel the love of the universe pervading her inside and out, that she was able to give up the excess food.

We begin to realize that our primary environment is not our family, or society, but the cosmos itself. This does not in any way undermine our sense of familial and social integrity or our enjoyment in the company of human beings. In fact, we are able to interact with the world with increased appreciation and effectiveness. But our sense of belonging in the world is integrated with, and surpassed by, a sense of belonging to something beyond, and in some sense more real and enduring, than the confusion of the world around us.

DHARMA: THE ETHICS OF FUNDAMENTAL CONSCIOUSNESS

Our true relationship with the universe contains an inherent ethical perspective. As we realize that our own essential being is also the essential being of all other life, we feel an underlying kinship with everyone we meet. When we know our self as the pervasive ground of life, we have learned the basic language of all beings, including animals and plants. In this shared field of fundamental consciousness, we do not need to adopt a static attitude of goodwill that obscures the richness of our feelings and the directness of our contact with ourselves and others. To actually experience the heart of a bird, or the aliveness of a tree, or the complex emotions in another person, evokes a spontaneous response of empathy and compassion.

There is also a more subtle manifestation of ethics in fundamental consciousness. This is expressed in the Sanskrit word dharma. In the Buddhist tradition, this word has several meanings. It refers to the Buddhist metaphysical understanding of the universe and enlightenment, the teaching of this understanding, and the living of this understanding. The direct translation of "dharma" is "justice." To live dharmically is to practice the justice of enlightenment. But this practice is not a preconceived set of behaviors. It is the alignment of oneself with the metaphysical functioning of the universe. It suggests that we are unified with the wisdom and love of the whole, and with the spontaneous unwinding toward enlightenment of all human beings. To the extent that we can act without artifice, without manipulation of ourselves and others, our actions are the actions of cosmic consciousness, the perfect tao. This means that our own truth benefits the truth of the life around us.

The idea that we can be aligned with the will of God also exists in Western religion. In Judaism, there is the concept of the mitzvah, which has a range of meaning from a good deed to a general attitude of justness and benevolence toward others. Jewish scholar Abraham J. Heschel (1959) writes, "Every act done in agreement with the will of God is a mitzvah" (p. 186). Hasidic writer Reb Zalman Schachter (1975) defines mitzvah as " . . . the divine will doing itself through the vehicle of the now egoless devotee" (p. 40).

Christian interpreter Maurice Nicoll (1967) writes, "When Good comes first, a man acts from mercy and grace. Then he is made Whole. When he is Whole, he no longer misses the mark" (p. 59). In this quote we have the idea that the individual becomes whole by being good. And the more subtle idea, very similar to the Buddhist idea of dharma, that he is now right on target, that he does not "miss the mark." That mark is the action that benefits everyone involved.

Epilogue

Above all else, the spiritual path is a process of becoming real. We grow toward internal contact with ourselves at the same time as we transcend our separateness and realize our oneness with everything around us. This includes the unfolding of our essential human qualities—awareness, love, and sensation. It requires the integration of love and detachment, distance and intimacy.

We cannot become real by pretending to be other than who we are right now. Even after we have begun our realization of fundamental consciousness, we are still incomplete, fragmented people, at the same time as we are attuned to the dimension of wholeness and unity. This means that we retain our human right to sing the blues, even though we are increasingly capable of joy and peace.

As our realization progresses, our desire for completeness grows stronger. Eventually it becomes central in our lives, the basis of our life choices, and the primary source of our satisfaction. In the modern world, as probably in all previous eras, the growing individual must swim against the powerful, hypnotic tides of ignorance and cynicism. Yet we ride the even more powerful, hidden current of the spontaneous process of enlightenment.

When we realize fundamental consciousness, we live in a dimension that is unknown to most people. We then have only our own perception and experience to guide and reassure us. We must trust the subtle signs that mark our own personal path toward wholeness—the deepening currents of energy in our body, the freedom of our love, the radiance in the air, the synchronicity between outer events and our inner needs, and the increasing transparency of our body and environment. Although religious affiliation is certainly an option, once we have entered the dimension of fundamental consciousness, there is no necessity for outward ritual or excessive discipline. The path emerges as we go, bringing us the circumstances and practices that we need in order to facilitate our growth. At the core of everyone and everything is radiant, unbroken consciousness, the root of the universe. When we live in this core, we experience the natural oneness of the body, the essential self, and the transcendent, all-pervasive ground of fundamental consciousness.

References

Almaas, A. H. (1986). *Essence*. York Beach, ME: Samuel Weiser Inc.

Blackstone, J. (2002). *Living Intimately*. London: Watkins Publishing.

Chodorow, N. (1978). *The Reproduction of Mothering*. Berkeley and Los Angeles: University of California Press.

Durckheim, K. G. (1962). *Hara*. London: Unwin Hyman Limited.

Freud, S. (1961). *Beyond the Pleasure Principle* (J. Strachey, trans.). New York: W. W. Norton & Company.

Gilligan, C. (1982). *In a Different Voice*. Cambridge, MA: Harvard University Press.

Hendrix, H. (1988) *Getting the Love You Want*. New York: Harper Perennial.

Heschel, A. J. (1959). *Between God and Man*. New York: Free Press.

Kapleau, P. (1980). *The Three Pillars of Zen*. Garden City, NY: Anchor Books.

Laing, R. D. (1965). *The Divided Self*. New York: Penguin.

Loori, J. D. ed. (2002). *The Art of Just Sitting*. Boston, MA: Wisdom Publications.

Lucador, W. V., H. Romer, & H. Walach (2007). "Synchronistic

Phenomena as Entanglement Correlations in Generalized Quantum Theory." *Journal of Consciousness Studies.* 14, no. 4, pp. 50–74.

Mahler, M. (1975). *The Psychological Birth of the Human Infant.* New York: Bantam Books.

Mindell, A. (1985). *Working with the Dream Body.* London and New York: Routledge & Kegan Paul.

Nicoll, M. (1967). *The New Man.* New York: Penguin Books.

Nikhilananda, S. (trans.) (1989). *Self-Knowledge.* New York: Rama krishna-Vivekananda Center.

Nishitani, K. (1983). *Religion and Nothingness.* Berkeley and Los Angeles: University of California Press.

Norbu, N. (1986). *The Crystal and the Way of Light.* New York: Routledge & Kegan Paul.

Rabjam, L. (1998). *The Precious Treasury of the Way of Abiding* (R. Barron, trans.) Junction City, CA: Padma Publishing.

Rabjam, L. (2001). *The Precious Treasury of the Basic Space of Phenomena* (R. Barron, trans.). Junction City, CA: Padma Publishing.

Rangdrol, S. T. (1993). *The Flight of the Garuda* (E. P. Kunsang, trans.). Kathmandu: Rangjung Yeshe Publications.

Reich, W. (1945). *Character Analysis* (V. R. Carfagno, trans.). New York: Touchstone.

Schachter, Z. (1975). *Fragments of a Future Scroll.* Germantown, PA: Leaves of Grass Press.

Shankaracharya, S. (1989). *Upadesa Sahasri* (S. Jagadananda, trans.). Mylapore, India: Sri Ramakrishna Math Printing Press.

Sharma, C. (1987). *A Critical Survey of Indian Philosophy*. Nagar, India: Motilal Banarsidass.

Singh, J. (trans.) (1979). *Siva Sutras*. Delhi: Motilal Banarsidass.

Stambaugh, J. (1999). *The Formless Self*. Albany: State University of New York Press.

Stern, D. N. (1977). *The First Relationship*. Cambridge, MA: Harvard University Press.

Stern, D. N. (1985). *The Interpersonal World of the Infant*. New York: Basic Books.

Trungpa, C. (1972). *Mudra*. Berkeley, CA: Shambhala.

Trungpa, C. (1988). *The Myth of Freedom*. Boston, MA: Shambhala.

Yuasa, Y. (1987). *The Body: Toward an Eastern Mind-Body Theory*. Albany: SUNY Press.

Index to the Exercises

1. Attunement to Fundamental Consciousness. 15

2. Seeing and Hearing with Fundamental Consciousness 23

3. Finding the Subtle Core of the Body 42

4. Qualities of Fundamental Consciousness 46

5. Experiencing the Quality of Self. 60

6. Releasing the Bound Fragments 77

7. Releasing Bound Attitudes 78

8. Relating from the Subtle Core 99

9. Letting Life Go Through 107

10. See with the Whole Eye 119

11. Touching with the Whole Body 119

12. Refining the Breath 121

13. Opening to the Upward Current 126

14. Balance. 127

15. Subtle Healing 129

16. Moving as Fundamental Consciousness 132

17. Cultivating a Relationship with the Cosmos. 140

18. Attuning to Oneness with the Cosmos. 141

Index

A

abuse, physical, 38, 67
abuse, sexual, 38, 80–81, 131
Almaas, A. H., 53–54, 70
Anna (patient), 39
authenticity, 3–5
awareness
  essence of, xv–xvi
self-knowing, 5

B

balance, 125, 129, 149, 150
Bella (patient), 48–49
binding, psychological, 64–81, 94.
  See also limitations, self-imposed
body, the. *See also* core, vertical
  inhabiting the internal space of,
    111–34
  transformation of, 116–18
bodywork, 76
breathing, 64, 121–23, 151
Buddha, the, 9, 151
buddhi, 71
Buddhism
  on breathing, 64
  Dzog-chen school of, 64, 151
  enlightenment in, 7, 8–9
  on fundamental consciousness,
    xv, 2, 3–4, 7–9, 44–45

on the illusion of separateness, 85
on the self, 28
selfless service in, 55
Tibetan, 28, 30, 41, 64,
  135–36, 148, 151
on visualization, 148
Zen, xiv, 5, 7–9, 20, 64, 114,
  151

C

chakras, 45, 102
channel, subtle, 41–45, 50, 76,
  99–101, 111
childhood, experiences from. *See
  also* infants, experiences of
  breathing and, 123
  God and, 152, 153
  healing and, 63–64, 72–75, 77,
    79–81
  intimacy and, 85, 86–88,
    89–90, 92–95, 96–97,
    98–99, 104
  physical sensation and, 131
  the senses and, 117
  stimulation and, 138–39
  synchronicity and, 144–46,
    147–48, 149
core, vertical
  balance and, 128
  contact with, 41–45, 50

healing and, 76
intimacy and, 85, 92, 94, 97–98,
    99–105, 110
kundalini and, 120
space outside the body and, 114
subtle channel and, 111
creativity, 148

D

desire, 148–49
detachment, 105–7
dharma, 155–56
distractions, 38
dreams, 150
Durckheim, Karlfried Graf, 153

E

ego, 52–53
embodiment, 111–34
EMDR (Eye Movement Desen-
    sitization and Reprocessing
    therapy), 150
energy, 120–21
    from core-to-core contact, 101–3
    deepening currents of, 158
    fundamental consciousness and,
        20–22
    gravity and, 125
    healing and, 130
    in letting life go through exercise,
        108, 109
    movement and, 131
    in Oriental medicine, 128–29
    refinement of the senses and, 116
    Reich on, 69

self and, 71
synchronicity and, 148
enlightenment
    description of, 1–25
    gradual vs. direct path to, 9
    misconceptions about, 5–11
    three thresholds of, 8–9
exercises
    attunement to fundamental
        consciousness, 15–19
    attunement to oneness with the
        Cosmos, 141
    balance, 127–28
    breathing, 121–23
    cultivating a relationship with
        the Cosmos, 140–41
    direct experience, 23–24
    experiencing the quality of Self,
        60–61
    healing, 129
    letting life go through, 107–8, 109
    moving as fundamental con-
        sciousness, 132–33
    opening to the upward current,
        126–27
    qualities of fundamental con-
        sciousness, 46–48
    releasing bound attitudes and
        fragments, 77–80
    seeing and hearing with funda-
        mental consciousness, 23–24
    seeing with the whole eye, 119
    subtle core, 42–44, 99–101
    touching with the whole body,
        119–20
existentialism, 104

experience. *See also* childhood,
    experiences from; infants,
    experiences of
direct, 12–15, 23–24, 106
imaginary, 85
peak, 7–8

F

faith, 153
flow, 106–7
Freud, Sigmund, 145, 146

G

Gilligan, Carol, 88
God, projections onto, 152–55
grace, enlightenment and, 6, 7
gravity, 124–25, 149–50
grief, 37, 40, 51, 66, 115, 145
growth, personal
    healing and, 130
    intimacy and, 83–86, 110
    spontaneity of, 150–51
    synchronicity and, 143,
        146–47, 148

H

healing process, 63–81, 128–30,
    143, 148
Hendrix, Harville, 146
Heschel, Abraham J., 156
Hinduism. *See also* yoga
    on buddhi, 71
    chakras in, 45, 102
    on fundamental consciousness,
        xv, 2, 3, 9–10

Kashmir Shaivism school of, 136
    on the self, 28, 40–41
    on the universe, 149
    Vedantic school of, 114–15, 136
    on the vertical core, 45
Hisamatsu, 44–45
hypervigilance, 94–95

I

identity, individual, 86–87
illness, 148
individuation, 86–91, 110
infants, experiences of. *See also*
    childhood, experiences from
    healing and, 63–64, 72–75
    intimacy and, 86, 87–88, 89–90, 93
    stimulation and, 138–39
intimacy, 83–110, 136

J

Journal of Consciousness Studies, 143
Judaism, 156

K

Kabir, 83
Kapleau, Philip, 151
kundalini, 120

L

Laing, R. D., 90–91
life, acceptance of, 7
limitations, self-imposed
    breathing and, 123
    the false self and, 52
    healing and, 64–69, 74–75

intimacy and, 84, 103
between parents and children,
    139–40
release of, 115
selflessness and, 28–30, 32
the senses and, 117
spontaneity and, 152
Living Intimately (Blackstone), 99
love, 10, 45, 49, 139, 158
Lowen, Alexander, 120

M

Mahler, Margaret, 86, 87, 88, 89,
    93, 95
meditation, 34, 64, 76, 114, 151
memory, repressed, 69–81, 151
mind,
    movable, 71
    ordinary, 7
    Yuasa on, 114
Mindell, Arnold, 145
misconceptions, about the body
    and enlightenment, 114–16
mitzvah, 156
movement, 131–33

N

narcissism, 34, 67, 104
Nicoll, Maurice, 156
Nishitani, 28
nobody, and somebody, 39–40
nonexistence, 27–31
Norbu, Namkhai, 135–36

O

object constancy, 86, 95. *See also*
    individuation

P

pain, emotional
    breathing and, 123
    the false self and, 50–52, 54–55
    fundamental consciousness and,
        56
    God and, 152
    gravity and, 150
    healing and, 64–75, 80–81
    intimacy and, 84–85, 89, 94,
        95, 99, 109–10
    the senses and, 117
    spontaneity and, 151
    synchronicity and, 142, 145,
        146, 148
parents, 96–97, 98–99, 104,
    138–39, 145–46, 152
patience, 113
Paul (patient), 48–49
Penelope (patient), 38–39
perception, direct, 116–17
person, and cosmos, 135–56
perspective, shortened, 93–94
Pierrakos, John, 120
Process Therapy, 145

R

Rabjam, Longchen, 2, 5
Ramakrishna, 153
reality, recognition of, 4
rebirthing, 150

Reich, Wilhelm, 69–70, 71, 72, 120
relating, to others, 91–105
relational style, learned, 96–99
relaxation, 150
repetition compulsion, 145, 146
Rilke, Rainer Maria, 14
Rinpoche, Chogyam Trungpa, 30, 151
Rolf, Ida, 70
Roshi, Maezumi, 5

S

Schachter, Reb Zalman, 156
self, 27–62, 94
    delusory nature of, xi
    essential, 35–50
    false, 50–55
    Stern on, 88
self-confidence, 134
self-esteem, 49–50
selflessness, 27–62
    ethical, 55–56
    logical, 56–58
    ultimate, 58–59
self-objectification, 95–96
self-possession, 37
Seng Chao, 13, 135
sensation, physical, 130–31, 139
senses, refinement of the, 116–18
separation, psychological, 32–33,
    85, 98–99, 104
separation-individuation process,
    86–91
sex, sexuality, 92, 102–3, 131, 134,
    153

Shankara, 2, 63, 136
Sharma, Chandradhar, 40–41
Sheng-yen, 9
Shikan-taza, 151
sleep, 150
somebody, and nobody, 39–40
speech, 123–24
spontaneity, 150–52
Stern, Daniel N., 51, 72, 87–88,
    89–90, 93, 138–39
stimulation, 138–40
subjectivity, elemental, 28
suffering, 40. *See also* grief; pain,
    emotional
sushumna, 41
synchronicity, 142–49

T

Teresa, Mother, 55
time, sense of, 92
transmission, direct, 139
truth, 156

U

unity, of enlightenment. *See also*
    universe, oneness with the
intimacy and, 83–84, 104–5, 110
non-fusion and, 35–37
normalcy of, 5, 11–12
perspective and, 56
the senses and, 116–17, 118
universe, oneness with the, 135–38,
    140–41, 149, 153, 154–56
unselfishness, 55

V

vision, 24–25
visualization, 148
voice, 124

W

"witness, the," xv

Y

yoga, 102, 120
Yuasa, 114